BUILD YOUR OWN
PATHS, STEPS & PATIOS

BUILD YOUR OWN
PATHS, STEPS & PATIOS

PENNY SWIFT AND JANEK SZYMANOWSKI

NEW HOLLAND

ACKNOWLEDGEMENTS

When a project like this draws to a close, there are always many people the authors need to thank. In particular, those who helped us with technical information, checked the manuscript, and allowed us to photograph their homes, as well as the corporations that assisted with the step-by-step projects, and friends and acquaintances who so willingly posed for the photographs.

Specific corporations to which we owe our gratitude are Corobrik, which produces facebricks and pavers, Smartstone, manufacturers of a range of reconstituted stone products, Terraforce, a leader in the field of earth-retaining systems, Klapmuts Concrete, which manufactures Terrafix blocks, and Kaytech Geotechnical and Industrial Fabrics, which introduced us to the fin-drain system. Several people in these companies deserve a special mention. These are Mike Ingram, regional director of Corobrick, South Africa, Andy van Niekerk of Smartstone, and Holger Rust who invented Terraforce retaining systems, which are now available worldwide.

Several consultants read the manuscript for accuracy, and our gratitude goes to all of them. A special word of thanks to Steve Crosswell, regional director of the Portland Cement Institute, who not only read and checked the text, but also gave us invaluable advice on numerous occasions.

Although we cannot make mention of every person, we are, however, grateful to all those people who allowed us to feature their homes in this book. Acknowledgements, also, to the people who posed for photography. In addition to co-author and photographer, Janek Szymanowski, who constructed several of the paths, steps, and patios, and who appears in a number of the photographs, we thank John Forbes, Paddy Kelly, and the late "Morgie" Morgan.

Finally, we acknowledge the assistance of the Struik team – editor Jenny Barrett, illustrator Clarence Clarke, designer Dean Pollard, and project coordinator Richard Pooler.

First published in the UK in 1996 by
New Holland (Publishers) Ltd
London • Cape Town • Sydney • Singapore

Reprinted 1997

24 Nutford Place, London W1H 6DQ, UK

PO Box 1144, Cape Town 8000, South Africa

3/2 Aquatic Drive, Frenchs Forest, NSW 2086, Australia

Distributed by Sterling Publishing Company, Inc
387 Park Avenue South, New York, NY 10016

Distributed in Canada by Sterling Publishing
C/o Canadian Manda Group, One Atlantic Avenue, Suite 105, Toronto, Ontario, Canada M6K 3E7

Copyright © 1996 in text Penny Swift 1996
Copyright © 1996 in photographs Janek Szymanowski 1996
Copyright © 1996 New Holland (Publishers) Ltd 1996

Editor Jenny Barrett
Editorial assistant Anita van Zyl
Designer Dean Pollard
Cover design Dean Pollard
Design manager Petal Palmer
Design assistant Lellyn Creamer
Illustrator Clarence Clarke
DTP conversion Dean Pollard and Darren McLean
American adaptation: American Pie, London, UK

Reproduction by cmyk prepress
Printed and bound by Tien Wah Press (Pte) Ltd, Singapore

ISBN 1 85368 589 5 (hb)
ISBN 1 85368 740 5 (pb)

CONTENTS

Paths, steps, and patios are found in just about every garden, regardless of its size. Not only are they practical features, providing a solid and safe route for pedestrians and offering a place to sit outdoors, but they are also useful landscaping "tools." A wide range of materials may be used to construct them and to create an effective outdoor style that will suit your living environment, your tastes, and your needs.

Functional factors usually come first, and irrespective of the type or size of your garden, designing any outdoor area is a creative challenge which demands patience and a practical approach. Paths, steps and patios are built from "hard landscaping" materials such as bricks, stone, and mortar, but they also rely on planting and other finishing touches to look attractive and enhance your outdoor scheme. Since gardens grow and constantly change with the seasons, it is essential to have a clearly defined idea before

you begin to create a basic plan or alter an existing layout. Before you start either planting or removing established plants and cutting down trees to accommodate a new walkway, flight of steps, or patio, consider all the options. You do not have to be a trained landscaper to succeed, but it helps to have a basic knowledge of plants, as well as an appreciation of the various elements that can be combined with them.

For practical reasons, it is always best to tackle the permanent elements of a garden first, and to create a basic layout which will allow for expansion and development later. Once you have laid paths, driveways, and patios, incorporating steps and terraces where necessary, and erected fences or walls, you can turn your attention to trees, shrubs, and flowers. After all, if plants are to be included in a patio design, or perhaps grown between stepping stones or in planters on a garden stairway, it makes sense to

complete all the messy structural work before you even start to prepare the soil for planting.

If, perhaps because of financial constraints, you cannot tackle all the building work now, it is usually quite possible to allow for later expansion and development of the plan (see page 10), but it is best to identify the position of future paths, steps, patios, and so on at an early stage.

Apart from their practical functions, which include not only providing easy access and a stable place to walk but also linking or dividing different areas of the property, pathways also have an esthetic role to play. If imaginatively laid out, they will add interest and charm to the garden, enticing one to follow the route that lies ahead, and they can provide visual and thematic continuity between various sections of the garden.

Whatever the size of your house and garden, the addition of a patio will extend your outdoor living space.

Natural rock forms a stepped path.

Cast concrete strips define the walkway next to an attractive brick-paved patio.

Originally, the patio was an inner courtyard which was open to the sky. Today patios may be sheltered or open, and sited alongside the house or built as a separate feature within the garden itself. The design possibilities are almost endless, especially if you consider including additional features which could enhance the outdoor area. For those who enjoy entertaining and cooking outdoors, built-in seating and a brick barbecue are practical additions, while pergolas and screens provide increased shelter and privacy. Water features and planters soften the effect of hard materials and make the visual transition between the built surface and the garden itself less abrupt.

Most patios are built adjacent to the house. There are usually several positions in which you can build such a patio, leading from different rooms or parts of the house. Alternatively, you may prefer to locate a paved area for entertaining in the heart of the garden. This could be a sunken section surrounded by trees, or a terrace overlooking the garden.

Many patios are not built at the same level as the house or garden, and so it is often necessary to construct steps for easy access. While this practical function will always be paramount, steps can still be pleasing to the eye, especially if you include planters, pillars, or flower beds on either side. Properly planned and imaginatively designed, they will be an attractive addition to any outdoor area.

This book will help you to plan and design a range of paths, steps, and patios, and offers guidelines on how to site a patio and lay out your garden to best advantage. Practical details and esthetic considerations are discussed, and there are many imaginative ideas and suggestions for new gardens, as well as for improving an existing layout.

Cost issues are examined and ways of quantifying various materials detailed. A wide range of materials is presented, helping to make your choice easier and more informed. There is advice on the relevant tools, and several construction methods are explained in detail.

The steps and porch have been tiled to create an authentic Victorian look.

Clearly illustrated step-by-step instructions show the principles behind laying paths and constructing patios and steps, using a few basic building methods. There is also a selection of plans, each of which includes a detailed materials list. The designs use a variety of materials including concrete cast *in situ*, timber poles, railroad ties, bricks, and stone. The designs range from rustic steps and paths to stylish brick-paved patios with formal stairways attached. All can be adapted to suit the constraints of your site. In some cases formal building plans will be necessary. You are advised to check with your local planning board before putting the plan into action.

Whether you are experienced in home improvement or a new homeowner with no experience at all, *Build Your Own Paths, Steps, and Patios* will arm you with a balance of inspiration and technical know-how, putting you in a position to tackle a variety of projects or to oversee those which you prefer others to complete for you.

Railroad ties used as steps.

Careful planning always pays off. If you know exactly what you want before you start building, particularly where you want to site the path, flight of steps, or patio and what materials you will need for the project, you will save time and money in the end, and avoid the frustration caused by a badly organized project.

The most obvious route for a path may be from the gate to the front door, but the biggest mistake could be to lay it out in a straight line that bisects a small front garden. Instead, the answer may be to move the gate, or to design a path that curves slightly around a natural feature such as a tree.

Start by identifying your needs and determining how these can best be accommodated in your garden scheme. For instance, should you establish a walkway from the front gate or parking area to the house? Is there a need for paths from the kitchen to service areas, or to a herb garden or vegetable patch? Are there sloping areas which would be easier to negotiate via steps of some sort? Do you want to increase outdoor living space by building a patio? Compare the various locations and layouts which may be suitable and then produce a thorough costing to ensure that the plan is actually viable.

PREPARATION

If your house is new and building work has just been completed, the first step to take before you start laying out any paths, steps, and patios is to ensure that all rubble has been removed. Earthworks may be necessary, and can include removal or relocation of large rocks and leveling the ground. If rocks are to be moved or dirt shifted, these tasks can be completed at the same time as the clean-up operation.

Regardless of the materials to be used, you should establish what kind of sub-base will be required and whether special steps will have to be taken to ensure that there is adequate drainage (see pages 35-36.)

Foundations

A solid foundation is essential for this type of garden work. If the ground is stable and level, the site will simply need to be cleared and a bed of suitable sand (see page 31) used to cushion the bricks, blocks, or paving slabs. However, you may need to compact or at least tamp the earth down firmly first, and if the ground is at all unstable, you should prepare a sub-base, or in some cases a solid concrete foundation.

If ground conditions and soil are problematic, or if the property slopes steeply, measures ought to be taken to ensure that pathways, steps, and patio floors do not subside. If you are not familiar with standard building practices, it is best to consult professionals for advice at this stage. Allow them to help you assess your site and recommend how to deal with it (see page 10.)

FUNCTION

Paths, steps, and patios are essentially permanent elements of the garden, and are part of the hard landscaping plan. Besides their most obvious functions, they also enable you to create a focal point for planting

Simple brick steps lead to the front entrance of a house.

and can be used to establish a particular theme in the garden. For this reason, it is essential to have a clear idea of what you want in the planning stages.

Patios

While patios are sometimes included in the plan of a house when it is built, many people add them only when they have lived in a house for some time. The design and style of your house and garden will help to determine the best location for a patio and the materials which will be most suitable for its construction. But it is also essential to examine your needs closely and to consider the primary reasons for having a patio.

A likely motive will be to create an outdoor living area or place for entertaining guests. However, you may want a secluded patio where you can relax away from the hustle and bustle of the house. Perhaps you want somewhere to sunbathe, or a solid paved area where children can play, or you can push strollers and carts within clear view of the house.

Once you have decided on the site of the patio, you can consider linking it to other outdoor areas by means of pathways and establish where these could be sited.

Paths, walkways, and driveways

You may want a path leading from the parking area, carport, or garage to the house, and invariably you will also need a pathway from the entrance of the property to the front door of the house. Additional walkways may well be necessary to provide easy access to areas or features within the garden – outbuildings, a swimming pool or ornamental pond, patio, herb garden, or washing line, for instance. In the larger garden, pathways may also be used visually to divide the lot by causing a break in the landscape, and by defining separate areas of interest or function. In the right environment, they may be built to flank grassed terraces or lawns, or to create an attractive and practical border alongside flower beds.

A change of materials from brick to slate demarcates a patio area.

Two strips of brick paving cut down costs on a long driveway.

Home improvements do not necessarily mean you have to do all the work yourself. Some home-owners favor the hands-on approach – especially when it comes to gardens – while others prefer to supervise other people doing the work, or to consult professionals and contract specialists to do everything for them, from design to construction, and even planting. The choice is yours.

If your house was designed by an architect, there is a good possibility that patios were included in the basic design, even if these were not initially built. Features such as driveways, swimming pools, patios and pergolas, and even garden walls, are often drawn on building plans but only built at a later stage when additional finances are available. Steps may also be included in the plan, but it is unlikely that garden paths would be shown. Whether this is the case or not often depends on local planning and zoning considerations. Some of the more obvious exceptions include substantial vertical walls, retaining walls, and long or steep external flights of steps, and in these instances, they may have to be built according to a civil engineering specification. A patio will often be indicated if the plans include a swimming pool, although this may not be necessary.

Check with your local building department and see what is required. You must ensure that no construction exceeds your property's boundaries – in fact, some local building codes require that you keep within specified building lines which fall inside your property's boundaries. If you need plans, an architect, designer, landscape architect, or draftsman will be able to help you.

Even if you are not required to have formal plans, you may want professional design assistance for paths, steps, and patios once the house is complete. You could approach the architect who designed your house, although it usually makes better sense to engage the services of a landscape architect or even a landscaper with a lesser qualification. These people are garden specialists and will be able to assist with planting as well as construction plans and guidelines.

Landscapers may undertake garden brickwork, paving, and so on, but it is best to enquire whether the person you are dealing with intends subcontracting the job or whether he or she has the resources to tackle the entire project. If not, you may be better advised simply to consult the landscaper concerned and employ a contractor or specialist company to do the building work for you. If you are prepared to liaise between the two, you are likely to save a substantial amount. In some areas, landscape contractors need a license to do residential work.

The other possibility for those who are not happy to lay bricks or throw concrete is to employ subcontractors. These people range from experienced pavers to unskilled laborers. Craftspeople generally have an hourly rate, while laborers will have a daily rate. Either way, negotiate the amount before work begins, in order to avoid any misunderstandings later on.

Whether you use a highly qualified landscape architect, a building or paving contractor, or subcontractors, make sure that you get references, preferably in writing, from previous clients, and check the quality of the work with some of the referees to ensure that you employ reliable and skilled people.

Other professionals you may want to consult are land surveyors, specialist engineers, and geotechnical experts. A land surveyor's report is useful if you are building on virgin land. An engineer's report will only be necessary if the site is problematic and contains large rocks or mabye clay. Use their services in the planning stages to save money later on.

Imprinting concrete to create a pattern is usually done by professionals.

Steep steps should only be built by someone with considerable experience.

The treads of these neat rendered steps are paved to match the brick path.

Unless a garage is situated on the boundary, it is almost always essential to have a driveway. There must be enough room to open car doors so that passengers can get in and out, and ideally it should be designed so that there is enough space to turn a car. You may want to extend the driveway to include a forecourt or turning circle. Unless there is adequate on-street parking for a second car and guests' cars, you could even consider creating an extra parking bay or two if space is not at a premium.

Steps

Wherever there are changes in level, paths inevitably incorporate steps or ramps. Often it is also necessary to build steps leading to entrances, providing access between terraces, and linking parts of the garden on sloping ground, even where formal pathways have not been created. Not only will an outdoor stairway neaten a trampled slope, but it will also encourage further exploration of the garden, as will a winding path that disappears from view.

LAYOUT AND LOCATION

The site chosen for a patio will probably be determined by the function you would like this area to perform, together with ease of access to and from the house and the view from the site. Paths and walkways, on the other hand, are usually laid out to link specific areas, and steps are sited where changes in level make them necessary. Since the size, shape, and topography of the property will also have a direct bearing on the plan, it is wise to work out everything carefully on paper first. It also helps to visualize the finished effect – wander around the garden and take note of both sunny and shady spots and the direction of prevailing winds, and remember that these will alter throughout the day and during the course of the year as the seasons change.

Consider all siting options carefully, and make an effort to see, for instance, which potential sites for a

A wooden walkway creates interest in a large garden.

patio have a good view and which might be exposed to the gaze of others.

A patio located alongside the living room can become an outdoor sitting room in good weather, while one sited outside a bedroom is more likely to become a private retreat, especially if it is screened in some way. If the house is rectangular, a large area leading off several rooms may be the ideal plan. However, your lifestyle may require several smaller, more intimate areas instead. Only you can decide.

If you have a site plan of the property, or if you can get one from the building department, make a copy of it to draw on. Otherwise, measure and mark out the boundaries as accurately as you can on a large sheet of graph paper, working to a scale of at least 1:200, and preferably 1:100. Show the position of the house and any outbuildings, as well as all other existing structures (pergolas, water gardens, arches, walls, fences, and anything else which is immovable) and natural features (large rocks, established shrubs, bushes, and trees, and any mounds or hollows). Make sure that you do not leave out any substantial feature.

Now draw in the patio areas and any other structures or features you are planning. These should include everything, from a swimming pool or tennis court to a planted kitchen garden or a children's play area. Also note service areas for hanging washing, storing garbage cans, making compost, and so on.

Then sketch in paths and walkways. These may, of course, be straight or winding, depending largely on whether there are any features they must detour around, the style of the garden, and the effect you wish to create (see pages 15-20.) The width will also be influenced by style, as well as function. A formal Victorian-style walk should be fairly wide, whereas a rustic garden path can be quite narrow. A driveway will need to accommodate cars and passengers entering and leaving the vehicles, and maybe a turning circle, and a parking bay or two.

Two railroad ties span a stream as part of a narrow, meandering pathway.

A large rock is retained as a feature at the bottom of these steps.

Open wooden steps lead up to the house from a timber walkway.

Wherever there is a change in level, between buildings or patios and the ground, steps are an obvious solution. If a path leads up a slope, you may want to introduce stairs for visual interest as much as for practical reasons. Like footways, steps may be built in a straight line or they may be curved, depending on the site and any particular style you want to adopt (see pages 16-20.) Dimensions should be in keeping with the pathways and entrances the steps lead to, but those constructed within the garden tend to be most effective when they are broad and gradual. A steep, narrow staircase can be an obstacle if one is taking a leisurely stroll about the garden, apart from which it might be dangerous in wet weather or at night.

MATERIAL OPTIONS

A wide variety of materials may be used to construct paths, steps, and patios. These range from solid or precast concrete to sliced logs, from bricks and blocks to old railroad ties. Some materials are more permanent than others, and each creates a different visual impression.

In many instances, it is possible to combine various materials for effect as well as convenience. For example, a simple stepping-stone path, created with precast slabs or sliced tree trunks, may join up with conventional brick steps leading to a brick-paved patio. A cobbled pathway might meander from a substantial stairway built from concrete cast *in situ*, while a flagstone and ground-cover path could connect timber decking with a slate-tiled patio. However, take care not to mix too many different surface materials, as the effect could become disjointed rather than interesting.

The materials you eventually decide to use is largely a matter of personal choice, although it is always best to complement those used to construct existing features elsewhere in the garden such as planters, barbecues, and garden walls, as well as the house itself.

The architectural style of the house and the materials used to create it are also important considerations which should not be overlooked (see pages 16-20.) The full range of possibilities for outdoor surfaces is discussed on pages 20-25. You may find that there are several different surfacing materials which are suitable for your garden plan. Weigh up the advantages and disadvantages of each, taking into consideration cost factors, safety, and ease of construction, before making a decision.

COUNTING COSTS

It is always vital to cost a project accurately before embarking on a building program. If you plan properly, you will be able to establish a budget you can live with. Inadequate planning often leads to delays and hitches which waste time and materials.

If you are going to do the work yourself, you will need to quantify materials and assess any additional costs. The main materials (paving bricks, concrete, precast paving slabs, and so on) are just one part of the cost factor. It is also important to price everything else required for building, from cement, sand, and stone, to drainage pipes, ducting, plants, and lighting accessories. Once you have decided which construction methods you are going to use, examine your tool kit and make sure you have all the tools required. If you plan to rent any tools, make allowance for the cost involved.

Digging holes for foundations, mixing concrete, and transporting heavy materials through the garden can be particularly arduous tasks. If you are likely to need assistance, include labor costs – even family members may demand pay! Finally, itemize the basic construction cost, finishes, lighting, planting, and so on, and complete the project in phases if necessary.Even if you intend to use professionals, even for part of the job, it is vital to avoid expensive mistakes and unnecessary wastage.

A raised patio alongside the house.

When designing patios and positioning paths, steps, and driveways, it is essential to aim for unity and harmony. The type of walkway or sitting area you choose must suit the house and the garden, and their proportions should be in keeping with the property as a whole.

Designing a garden can be a daunting task, particularly if you are starting from scratch. It is also a time-consuming business which demands patience and persistence. Paths, steps, and patios form a kind of skeleton within the garden, and along with boundary walls, buildings, and any existing features, are all part of the basic design of any outdoor area. An understanding of the basic principles of design is therefore essential. You will also need to take local weather conditions and the microclimate of your garden into account, not only when planting, but also when choosing the materials for constructing any outdoor features. This does not mean that you have to be a horticulturist or landscape specialist to succeed. With enthusiasm and imagination, a tremendous amount can be achieved.

The first step is to put the basic plan on paper (see pages 11-12.) This will give you a clear idea of how much land you have to work with, how the outdoor space is to be subdivided, and where all the elements will be sited. The next phase is to consider the many design details which will enable you to create your outdoor haven.

Decide what effects you would like to create and what materials you should use in which areas. Ask yourself whether you are going to keep to a particular style and whether you want to achieve a particular visual theme. If there are problem areas (these may include embankments and steep slopes, rocks, swampy spots, and so on), it is essential to decide at the outset whether special construction of terraces, decking, steps, and any other features will be necessary.

Although plants are a vital part of the plan, at this stage it is simpler to think purely in terms of color, size, and shape rather than specific species.

When it comes to putting the plan into action, the main question will be what to do first and how to stagger the various stages of the project. There are always countless options, but the best solution is to tackle the job systematically. Just as structural alterations should be tackled before you begin decorating inside your home, any construction work in the garden should ideally be completed before planting gets under way.

You will want to establish a basic framework, but if you cannot afford

An attractive patio designed to create an indoor-outdoor flow.

to lay paths and build patios at this stage, mark the areas where these features will eventually be located. Although you may decide to lay lawn or even plant flowers here for the time being, you will not want shrubs or trees to establish themselves if they will have to be removed later on.

THE BASICS

Paths and patios must be designed to suit the purpose they are to serve. It helps to think of the garden as a large outdoor room. Instead of carpeting, tiles, and so on, you have a range of surfacing options from grass and gravel to brick paving, flagstones, and concrete, some of which may also be used indoors. Inside you can introduce color and texture with fabric and paint. Outside, plants, flowers, and the materials chosen to surface your garden "floor" will do this for you.

The way you decide to combine these elements will go a long way towards determining the ambience of the garden as a whole. You will need to decide whether you want the effect to be wildly colorful or quietly restful, whether you are going to aim for a cosy private patio which offers solitude, or an open outlook which is not blocked by screens and tall plants, or intersected by walkways.

You may have decided to divide the outdoor space into a series of "rooms" linked by paths. These may be quite distinct from one another, and different in design. There may even be various types of path. However, it is still important to aim for harmony and to establish an overall sense of balance and proportion. Remember that even a seemingly chaotic, wild garden, with rough gravel paths and informal seating areas, often needs to be carefully planned and laid out.

TYPE

The type of garden you plan to create (and the individual features you choose to make up the garden) will involve a basic design decision, namely whether you want it to be formal or informal, beautifully symmetrical, or attractively irregular in character.

Rendering and painting these steps adds style to the garden.

A path using a blend of materials.

Gravel can be inexpensive, but effective.

The formal garden is generally characterized by straight lines, although circular paths may also be included in the scheme. Wide walkways, rigid planting, and grand staircases are at home here, along with terraces and courtyards. Symmetry and balance are the two essential distinguishing features of the formal garden.

Paths and patios are made from similar materials, usually relatively sophisticated, and neatly finished off. Marble, for instance, was a favorite in the great classical gardens, but slate, brick, and tile are equally appropriate.

Steps are usually built of brick, concrete, or planed lumber, often with pillars and balustrades on either side.

The informal garden uses rustic materials and curved, irregular lines and forms. Herbaceous borders alongside paths, with plants spilling over the edges, are perfect, as are stepping-stones which wander off around corners.

Materials chosen should be less contrived and with a casual, countrified look. Gravel and fieldstone paths are common, while steps are often built of rough stone. If bricks or concrete blocks are used, they should be laid to enhance the informal approach, and plants could also be encouraged to take root in the joints.

Of course, few things in life are as well defined as this, and in practice, many gardens include both formal and informal elements. This usually works best on a large spread, where sections can easily be subdivided, but even in a reasonably small area, you could combine these two types and establish, for instance, an informal planted area with a winding pathway, which leads to a relatively formal patio built adjacent to the house.

THEME

Professional designers often choose to follow a theme. This can work well, but it is essential to ensure that paths, steps, and areas intended for entertaining are appropriately designed and constructed. Style is an obvious theme (see below), one which usually relies on the existing architecture of the house. For instance, a cobblestone path will not suit a clean-lined modern house, and a marble-tiled patio could look quite out of place next to a brick or clapboard farmhouse.

If you decide to focus on color, you may want to use several shades of a chosen hue (a pink theme could range from deep cerise to soft powder-puff pink, while a blue theme could include lilac and purple tones) or you might prefer to mix colors. Perhaps your living room has been decorated in bold blues and yellows. If so, the obvious hues for a patio leading from this room will mirror the interior. This could change to yellow and orange along a linking pathway which disappears behind a screen wall or hedge into a herb garden. Here, the colors would be primarily yellow, orange, and blue, without too much planning on your part. This does not mean that surface materials need to match. In fact, it is probably more important to ensure that they complement established plants. There are always many possibilities, but a black slate patio could be very effective surrounded by blue and yellow flowers, while red brick shows up white blooms to good advantage.

Your theme may follow through the entire outdoor area, or it may be limited to one section only. Herbs and roses, for instance, are often planted in separate areas which are frequently bounded by paths.

STYLE

If the architecture of your house is distinctive, it makes sense to aim for a similar look in the garden, with paths and steps following a complementary pattern. Certainly a severe, formal layout will not suit a New England farmhouse, and a wild garden, intersected by winding gravel paths, will usually not complement the precise lines of an antebellum mansion. However, you do not need to have a 19t-century house to create a Victorian-style garden, or a Mission villa for a Mediterranean-style garden.

Steps and patios built from recycled bricks complement the Victorian style of the house.

Stepping stones lead through a small garden to a utility room.

A grass walkway reminiscent of the English country garden style.

A Japanese approach makes use of stone and pebbles.

Paths, steps and patios go back a long way in history. It is fascinating to learn what treatments were popular in the past, and even if you do not want to achieve a traditional effect, you may gain inspiration from previous centuries.

It is known, for instance, that stairways were seldom used as decorative elements in gardens before the 16th century. The Romans certainly built steps, but usually merely to allow access between various levels. In many large Italian Renaissance gardens, however, when design reverted to an essentially classical form, grand stairways were often introduced as a focal point. These frequently included imposing features, such as impressive balustrades and railings, fountains, and statuary. Elsewhere in Europe and Britain, garden steps gained less prominence, but they were still used to good effect. Even after the impact of the great 18th century landscape gardeners (including Capability Brown who replaced many a carefully planted formal garden with vast "natural" landscapes), they continued to have both an esthetic and a practical purpose.

Prior to the landscape movement, formal garden styles predominated throughout the Western world. Paths were usually straight, leading directly from one spot to another; the exceptions were perfectly circular routes and some rather unusual serpentine mazes. Then, predictably, there was a reaction against formality, and this reaction resulted in excessively winding pathways.

At the same time, the trends in oriental gardens were rather different. In early China, gardeners favored the meandering path, with its curves laid out to resemble an unrolling scroll. Often the route these paths took covered quite a distance as they threaded their way around rocks and large mounds (or mounts), the philosophy being that it is more enjoyable to travel than to arrive. Long, covered, open-sided walkways, known as *lang*, were also popular among the aristocracy in ancient China. These incorporated balustrades, elaborate latticework, and tiled roofs, and followed the contours of the ground, crossing water as bridges where necessary.

In Japan the approach to pathways was generally more natural, stepping-stones being strongly featured .

Traditionally patios were part of the building, created as atriums and courtyards which were usually paved and often featured a pool or pond. This probably had more to do with design and the desire for privacy than with the need for protection from intruders or enemies. The idea persisted for centuries. During the Middle Ages, the peristyles of the earlier Romans reappeared as cloisters and during the Italian Renaissance, as colonnaded courtyards.

In recent times, the patio has become loosely redefined as a place where garden and house meet. Its function and character, however, have continued to

grow, and the term is now used to refer to virtually any uncovered or partially covered outdoor area with a hard surface which is used for sitting or entertaining.

The materials used for steps, paths, and patios are the same in many cases, and these have not changed much over the centuries. The requirement has always been for a durable, hard surface which is both easy to maintain and visually attractive. Concrete-like materials have always been common, as have bricks and tiles, although the technology has obviously advanced considerably over the centuries. In Pompeii, a kind of concrete was made of pounded tile mixed with lime. Bricks have always been made from clay. Cut and random flagstones were also common for both garden and indoor use in areas where suitable stone occurred naturally.

Pebbles, too, have been a popular surface material for paths, patios, and courtyards. Pebble pavements were created by the ancient Chinese civilizations, and the Greeks used them both indoors and out, creating geometric and abstract patterns. Pebbles were set in wet clay soil. Nowadays, mortar can be used for setting cobblestones, and stones of different hues can be used to create patterns.

Tiles were also used in the earliest known gardens. In Persia, paths and even pools were tiled with mosaic to introduce color and pattern. In Moorish Spain, decorated tiles were used for steps and edgings, on walls, and around pools and fountains.

Slate and fieldstone are used successfully in an Italian-style garden.

Gravel is a good material to use to achieve an oriental look.

The important point is to aim for harmony in every possible way.

While fashion affects gardens as much as it does interiors and clothes, the 20th-century Western garden, perhaps more than any other, has constantly borrowed from other times and places. People have been making gardens for thousands of years, and there is much that we can learn from history. Indeed, anyone striving to achieve an authentic look should imitate surface finishes, period features, and structures as closely as possible, and should try to reproduce similar patterns of planting. Research your chosen style and do not be afraid to copy what you see.

Accepted garden styles range from a period look to the exotic. Some of the most popular include those which are reminiscent of the grand, formal European (and, in particular, Italian) gardens of the Renaissance, those which seek to evoke the timeless qualities found in certain famous English country gardens, and, of course, the Victorian approach.

Renaissance

While the origins of this style can be traced back to ancient Rome, it is the large, centuries-old Italian villas that give us much of our inspiration. Many of these gardens have been restored to their former glory and a number of them are open to the public. Of course, few people today have spreads this vast, but ideas can often be scaled down quite successfully.

In essence, the look is classically formal, with symmetrical pathways and grand stairways leading to balustraded terraces. There is very little color, but structures and statuary abound.

The modern interpretation involves a geometric layout with an abundance of paving. Various materials are suitable, since walkways of the genre were often of grass and gravel, and pathways and patios were made using any material from marble to fieldstone or pebble mosaic. Ideally, you should lay patio surfaces to form bands and panels of different colors and textures.

Oriental

Oriental gardens, both past and present, provide an extensive source of inspiration. Historically, the Chinese have been more flamboyant than the Japanese, and their long tradition of garden-making is unlikely to be matched. Ideally, one should have a thorough understanding of the ancient culture to interpret it correctly, but there are elements anyone can introduce to create an Eastern feel successfully.

Outdoor spaces are usually divided into a series of enclosures which are intended to be viewed independently. According to traditional Chinese belief, evil influences travel in straight lines, so pathways invariably wind and courtyards are sheltered and private. There is a focus on natural elements and both water and stone are symbolic.

Reconstituted stone and pebbles laid in concrete are quite acceptable materials in this style of garden, and it is also appropriate to tile or pave the floors of patios and terraces.

The simplicity and serenity of the Japanese approach, particularly that established by Zen Buddhists, is one which appeals to modern tastes. Designs are asymmetrical, with winding stepping-stone paths, gravel walkways, and pebble "rivers of life." Low-maintenance materials are a common feature, with stone, granite, or even concrete slabs forming both path and patio surfaces. Lumber decking often leads from the house itself.

Cottage

The tradition of the English cottage garden is quite specific, although it is difficult to attain an authentic style in the U.S., due to the different climate. The style developed out of necessity, with a profusion of flowers for the vase mixed with vegetables, herbs, and even fruit trees. There were no lawns or empty spaces and certainly no place for patios or swimming pools. All the available ground was cultivated, and paths and steps had a strictly functional purpose.

To a large extent, it is the pathways which give shape to the cottage-style garden. There is invariably a main path from the garden gate to the front door, as well as several secondary paths which provide access to the many plants. While these usually curve slightly, creating an informal impression, the route is reasonably direct.

It is not surprising that cottagers originally used local materials for surfacing their paths – these were obviously the least expensive. Well-trodden earth, stone, and gravel will all, therefore, fit the picture. In the contemporary cottage garden, brick, wood, and concrete slabs may also be used, but they should be artificially weathered to age the surface. There are many of ways of doing this, such as rubbing substances like manure or yogurt over the surface, sowing seed

in gaps, and simply encouraging moss and fungi to grow by providing constant moisture.

Scale and style should be carefully considered when steps are built. Keep construction simple and match materials with those used for pathways. Step slopes with logs, railroad ties, or even concrete lintels, backfilling with soil to secure them.

Victorian

If the Victorian interior was cluttered and fussy, so too were the gardens of this era. Strong and varied colors and a busy layout are the order of the day, while arbors, gazebos, arches, tunnels, and elaborate plant supports are found on patios and within the garden. The Victorians favored formal rose walks and pathways which led to arbors and retreats. Herb gardens, divided by paths leading to a central sundial, were another common feature, as were fussy carpet beds planted to imitate mosaic. Strong color

contrasts were popular for carpet bedding, which involved planting low-growing flowers, ground covers. and plants with colored foliage to create formal patterns. The plants you choose will depend on what is available locally, but some particularly suitable species include ornamental kales and cabbages, begonias, dwarf marigolds, and thyme.

Brick, grass, and gravel paths are suitable for this style, and patios may be surfaced in brick or fieldstone. If you have a porch or stoop which you use for outdoor living, the obvious surface finish is elaborate encaustic tiles. If you cannot source copies of authentic Victorian tiles, it is possible to achieve a similar look by laying tiles of several different colors to form geometric patterns.

For a Mission or Creole look, wrought-ironwork may be incorporated along paved terraces or as balustrades for garden stairways.

Even modern tiles can help you to give a patio a Victorian look.

A walkway of cleverly laid clay tiles leads to a patio featuring ceramic tiles.

Period-style pergolas are common along walkways and on patios, and arbors are often constructed to shade seating in the garden. Encourage moss to grow, and plant flowers that will seed themselves between the bricks, stones, concrete, and other materials used for paving and steps.

Mediterranean

Suitable where the winters are mild, this style evokes images of the Mediterranean region, rather than a particular era. Walled courtyards and patio gardens, typical of those found in Moorish Spain, provide privacy and shade and offer an opportunity to introduce varied themes.

The classical Mediterranean garden was formal and based on the teachings of Islam. Two canals often divided a rectangular courtyard in four, symbolizing the Rivers of Life and creating an intimate oasis (or paradise.)

There are a lot of "hard" surfaces in the Mediterranean garden and this is where container planting comes into its own. Just about any paving material will suit the style, from concrete to textured tile, but terracotta tiles and clay bricks are particularly appropriate. A popular option for paths and steps is to set cobblestones or smooth pebbles into concrete, creating patterns and motifs with varying shades of brown, gray, and white. Covered patios may be surfaced with ceramic tiles (make sure that they are the nonslip variety), since these were a feature of both Moorish and old Portuguese gardens.

SURFACE MATERIALS

The one feature almost all paths, steps, patios, and driveways have in common is a tough, durable surface. The material chosen will depend on several factors, including the role of each area, the type of garden you are planning, and a style you may want to recreate. A selection of materials appropriate for the more popular styles is on pages 22-25 and 28-32. Consider these along with the other elements. For instance, a purely functional path leading to the front door should be surfaced with a non-slip material. It

A meandering crazy-paving path.

English Country

Well defined within the house, this style takes its lead outside from famous English gardeners such as Gertrude Jekyll and Vita Sackville-West. Here there is a romanticism which defies description, one of the best examples being Vita Sackville-West's celebrated gardens at Sissinghurst in Kent, England.

Just as the interiors embody a timeless feeling of gracious living, so do the gardens of this genre. Surfaces have a patina of natural weathering which has allowed moss and lichen to take a hold. Paths and steps are charmingly overgrown, with plants breaking all straight lines as they tumble from borders and crevices, often growing between stones and bricks. Gravel, grass, stone (including reconstituted stone), and old bricks are all suitable materials.

When one is faced with a steeply sloping garden, the wooden deck becomes an excellent alternative to the conventional paved patio. Not only does this form of construction enable home-owners to add outdoor living space to the house, but it also creates the opportunity to reclaim land which might otherwise be unusable. Where rocky ground cannot be easily flattened, or in areas where the soil becomes waterlogged in wet weather, it is also a very useful option.

Decking has many other benefits and is certainly not for difficult sites only. Indeed, a timber deck raised just above the ground will provide an attractive, low-maintenance surface for year-round use in just about any garden. It may be built as an alternative to the conventional porch, either at ground level or extended from an upper story, or it may be erected around a swimming pool, spa or hot-tub, a pond, or even a tree-house or play structure.

A garden which slopes slightly may be the ideal site for multilevel decking. This could create the feel of terracing, or it may simply produce a series of separate but adjacent areas for sitting, playing, or entertaining. Designed so that each consecutive deck adjoins at an angle, multilevel decking can be a particularly impressive feature, and the slats produce an attractive pattern.

Sometimes timber decking is best used in conjunction with other paving or landscaping materials. A deck built alongside the house could lead down wooden steps to a brick-paved patio, or it could extend from an established patio beside the house, adding to the outdoor living space and possibly reclaiming a nearby slope.

Just as a patio will benefit from additional features, so too will a deck. An overhead structure of some kind will offer shade, while built-in seating, storage, and perhaps even simple tables or worktops will immediately increase its usefulness. Railings will add detail and increase the safety of a deck, while screens (latticework is popular) will give you added privacy and shield the area from wind.

Although timber decking suits most house styles, it is particularly appropriate for Japanese-style architecture and similar landscaping approaches. It also blends well with informal gardens.

Various methods are used for building decks, most of which will be within the capabilities of a competent home handyman. Most are built with sturdy upright supports of lumber or brick (which keep the decking above ground), and planed (milled) decking slats resting on an arrangement of beams, joists, and ledges.

The lumber used to construct a deck will depend on which suitable types are sold in your area. Although not always available, and expensive in some places, Californian redwood is one of the traditional choices, since the heartwood has a natural resistance to decay. Most decking woods should be pressure-treated before you buy them, and sealed and treated regularly to avoid infestation and rot, though some, like teak and balau, can simply be oiled or allowed to weather naturally. It is also important to use galvanized cleats, brackets, and screws to avoid the problem of rust, because rusting is not only unsightly, it also weakens the structure.

An attractive deck built over a steep slope increases usable space.

A low-level deck in the garden is used for entertaining and outdoor meals.

the chips scatter easily, especially in high winds or when walked on. The visual effect of bark chips is similar to that of gravel, and they should only be used in informal parts of a garden.

Brick

Perhaps more than any other paving material, brick can be used in just about every possible type and style of garden. It has been used for centuries, and in some parts of the world brick paths estimated to be more than 4,000 years old are still in use today.

Concrete and clay bricks and thinner pavers are available in a wide range of colors and may be laid in a multitude of patterns (see page 39.) The most common configuration is probably running bond (a simple grid formation), and the strongest, which is particularly suitable for driveways, is herringbone, laid either at right-angles or diagonally to the edge of the paving. Although a wall should never be built without the bricks interlocking, a simple stack bond (jack-on-jack) pattern, which involves no overlapping of bricks, is quite acceptable for level paving. Circular patterns are also popular for patio and driveway surfaces. Interlocking pavers are perfect for any surface which will be driven on, while "hard lawn systems," a relatively new range of products, comprise interlocking paving blocks which, when laid, leave spaces for planting.

Bricks and paving blocks may be laid on sand or a solid concrete slab with sand or mortar between them.

Cobblestones and setts

There is a certain fairytale romanticism about a narrow cobbled path, but it is important to consider practical factors before laying one in your own garden. The real thing consists of numerous rounded stones, often salvaged from river beds, pressed into mortar. They are not always easy to walk on and certainly not easy to balance chairs and tables on for patios.

A less expensive compromise, although not always as natural in effect, is to use more regular reconstituted stone or concrete setts, manufactured

Asphalt is a practical and relatively inexpensive surface for driveways.

A brick path between herbaceous borders.

Bricks used to create flowing lines.

should also take a short route and be well lit at night. On the other hand, a leisurely garden path leading to a bench with a view may a little less practical, as it will probably be less used , especially in the rain and dark.

Asphalt

Ideal for driveways, asphalt is generally regarded as a low-cost material and is seldom considered suitable for either paths or patio surfaces. Like tarmac, it is either rolled on by specialist

contractors while hot, or applied cold. The cold-mix variety is aimed at the home improvement market and is relatively simple to lay on a compacted sub-base. It is, however, not as hard-wearing as asphalt which is hot-rolled.

Bark chips

Suitable for play areas, as they allow a nice soft landing for children, and for mulching, bark chips are also favored in some places as a surface material for paths. A major disadvantage is that

These brick steps are topped with concrete treads.

Fine gravel is combined with stone in the Japanese manner.

in imitation of the original granite setts (which were cut from stone.) These are not as labor-intensive to lay as rounded cobblestones and are fairly regular in size and shape, creating a much more even surface on which to walk.

Concrete

One of the least expensive and most unimaginatively used materials is concrete. Perhaps because it is considered "cheap," people are generally uninventive when using it, yet simply by combining concrete with other materials and planting around it, it is possible to create patios, paths, steps, and driveways which have a very special charm and character.

Concrete is available in numerous precast forms – rounded, square, and rectangular slabs, kerbstones, reconstituted stone products, and even precast concrete ties may all be used to great effect and can be laid in a number of ways. Square slabs can be used to create a checkerboard effect, alternating the concrete with herbs or a fragrant ground cover, rounded shapes may be laid as stepping-stone pathways, and precast kerbs may be used either to create steps or to raise a patio on a level piece of ground (see pages 42-45.)

Concrete cast *in situ* is probably handled with even less sensitivity by the amateur builder. Sometimes, many square yards of ground are covered with the material and paths cast in long strips above the surface of the soil. Instead, concrete should be handled as a useful part of the design plan. Age the finished surface if you like this effect (see page 19), and allow it to blend in with your environment.

Gravel

Gravel is an inexpensive option, and is useful for paths and walkways in the garden. It is also an acceptable material for level driveways and parking areas, and very effective when used in conjunction with paving slabs. As it is naturally loose, gravel may also be spread over flowerbeds or between the clipped hedges of ornamental knot gardens. It helps to control weed growth and retain moisture in the soil.

It is essential to compact the earth beneath this material thoroughly and to contain it with some sort of edging to prevent it from spilling into flower beds and spreading onto the adjacent grass or paving.

The type of gravel you use will depend on what is available in your area. Material sold for use as sub-base under driveways is suitable, otherwise you can ask for the smallest single-sized crushed stone. You will need a much finer grade than is used for making concrete. If available in your area, pea gravel is the best choice.

Another possibility well suited for walkways is laterite, although it is not universally available. This material consists of a mixture of gravel and clay which is moistened with water and rolled to a smooth surface.

A few specialist companies offer pebble paving, which is made by bonding gravel-like stones in a mixture of resin and cemen. This is then applied over concrete to form a continuous surface.

Grass

Although grass eventually becomes worn down by constant foot traffic, it is sometimes the best choice for paths and walkways. Choose a tough variety and be prepared to mow, feed, and water it and generally to attend to its needs. Although people often neglect their lawns, grass should not really be regarded as a low-maintenance surface.

When it comes to patios, most people prefer, for practical reasons, to have a good, solid surface underfoot. Grass is, however, a reasonable temporary solution for some, and it can also be used as a more permanent material in combination with hard surfaces such as stepping-stones.

Stone

Real stone slabs look wonderful in any garden, either as a patio or terrace surface, or as a pathway. They are also a good natural material to choose for steps, especially if they are sited alongside a stone wall. While steps may be built with slabs or with rocks (provided they have at least one flattish side), patios and walkways should be laid with flat, solid flagstones or fieldstones.

Like other types of stone, slate is available in regular and irregular shapes, and may be laid as tiles or fieldstone. It is suitable for paths, patios, and the treads of steps. The dark charcoal-gray reconstituted stone tiles which are available in some areas can look remarkably like slate.

As natural stone is often difficult to come by, reconstituted stone (made by casting and compressing concrete in special molds) is a good alternative. Sizes are varied and shapes usually reasonably regular, making them a good choice for the amateur.

Tiles

A wide variety of tiles may be used on patios. You may be able to continue a ceramic tile surface used in the interior of your home, but it is generally advisable to ensure that any area exposed or even partially exposed to the elements should be frostproof and have a nonslip matte finish. Manufactured quarry tiles, handmade terracotta tiles, as well as those made from terrazzo (a mixture of colored marble and stone chips bedded in mortar) are all popular options that are particularly well-suited to the garden as their colors and textures blend in beautifully with those of nature.

If you are in any doubt as to whether a tile is suitable for your purposes, contact the manufacturer before buying the materials. Tiles are liable to crack in earthquake-prone zones.

Lumber

Apart from being the most common decking material, lumber is often used for steps and sometimes to surface both paths and patios as well. Sliced tree trunks provide an inexpensive material for stepping-stone pathways, although they become slippery, sometimes treacherously so, in wet weather. If you lay a large expanse of them, for instance in a parking area, aim for a slightly uneven upper surface to give tires a grip. Old railroad ties, made from tough hardwoods, are also well suited for surfacing paths and small patios (if you can find enough to cover a large surface.) They also make very unusual steps and may be used, together with other materials and

Sliced tree trunks in an informal, rambling garden.

plants, for attractive pathways. Debarked logs, which do not need to be perfectly rounded in shape, are also good material for informal steps. Backfilled with earth and laid across the front of each tread, they will provide a good footing up a natural slope. When used for decking, lumber is almost always sawn and planed (or dressed) to a good, smooth and attractive finish.

EDGINGS

Absolutely essential around most types of patio, edgings are also a necessity along the sides of pathways and walkways, and without them, driveways would inevitably collapse as cars ride over the edges. But an edging can also have esthetic value. It is possible to be imaginative and creative while ensuring that paving bricks, slabs, and so on are held in place, and loose materials prevented from spilling out onto adjacent surfaces.

If you have an old-fashioned garden, lay tiles on edge along pathways. If you prefer a more modern approach, a row of bricks may be laid at an angle to retain the surface material. Brick-paved paths and patios are usually edged with the same brick, laid at a slight angle for drainage, although precast concrete edgings (including special kerbstones) are also useful.

SCREENING AND SHELTER

Although not always strictly necessary, pergolas and awnings will offer some protection from the elements and increase the usefulness of any patio. Overhead structures could also be useful over walkways where they lead from a garage or parking bay, or link a gate to the front door.

Of course the roofing material of any pergola or overhead structure will determine the degree of shelter offered. Awning material (including shadecloth), canvas, and wood will give some shade, but will not prevent you from getting wet. If the motivation for building a pergola over a patio or walkway is to keep the area beneath it dry, then you will need to choose a more solid covering, like fiberglass,

polycarbonate, or even tiles, and the basic structure will therefore need to be more substantial to carry the weight of the roofing material.

Screening, on the other hand, is usually erected as a windbreak or to make a patio more private. It can

also be used to define or divide an area. Screen walls, plants climbing up trelliswork, or hedges alongside a pathway may be incorporated as design elements, defining the route as well as offering some protection.

Materials chosen for pergolas and

Bricks set at an angle to form an edging.

A pebble-paved surface edged in brick.

Once they have matured, plants grown over a pergola will offer shade from the sun.

screens should complement those used in the rest of the garden. Although materials may differ in appearance, the basic construction principles are similar for many of them.

LIGHTING

When it comes to garden lighting, the illumination of paths, steps, driveways, and patios should be top of the list. Not only does lighting extend the usefulness of these outdoor areas, but it is essential for general safety and security as well. Steps can be particularly hazardous at night, and corners where intruders could lurk in the dark are potentially dangerous, especially in and near parking and entrance areas. If a patio is not illuminated at night, its usefulness will be severely limited. While you are taking the time and effort to construct such an area, it makes sense to ensure that you can use it after dark, as well as during the day.

Lighting also adds to the decorative scheme outdoors. Used to highlight features alongside pathways and on patios, it lends character and charm to any garden.

Of course, the installation of electric lighting will usually involve enlisting the services of an electrician, unless you can utilize existing sockets and light fittings. This is often an option when a patio is created alongside the house. Unless a floodlight attached to the house adequately illuminates a pathway or driveway, it is usually necessary to lay suitable waterproof cabling underground.

Although you may be able to lay the cables and fix the fittings yourself, it is essential to employ a qualified person to connect up the wiring to the mains. Once underground wiring is in place, make sure that anyone working in the garden knows where it is, to prevent accidental damage with spades and other sharp tools.

It is worth noting that low-voltage lighting systems suitable for installation by the home handyman are available, and these have the added advantage of being much safer than standard installations.

Well-lit stairs lead from the entrance to the house.

Many lights and lamps are suitable for use outdoors, but it is essential that only sealed units are chosen. Although freestanding lamps and pillar-mounted fittings are useful alongside paths, it is best to aim for a good, general light on the patio. Wall-mounted lamps usually cast a warm glow over the entire area, while spotlights may be used to brighten a specific section of the patio, perhaps one used for outdoor eating. Uplighters are effective alongside steps, and floodlights will brighten a large area.

SEATING

Seating arrangements are found in most gardens. Some seats are fixed, others moveable, depending largely on function, where the furniture is sited, and what it is made of. Although the patio is the most obvious place to sit outdoors, paths may lead to a spot with a good view or even to a

focal point of the garden, and this is a good place to have a bench. If there is some sort of overhead shelter, an arbor or patio roof for instance, freestanding furniture is usually a practical option. If not, it may be preferable to consider built-in seats and tables, or even natural elements such as logs or planted earth banks.

On a patio, built-in seating can be a real boon; it can be left where it is in all weather conditions, all year round, and simply "dressed" with cushions when you want to use it. Various materials are suitable for permanent designs, although brick and stone are probably the most usual and the most versatile. It is more cumbersome to cast concrete *in situ* than to lay bricks, but the latter can be an expensive option. Lumber is another popular choice, but it is often better suited to decks than to patios.

Of course, some types of moveable furniture may also be left permanently in place. Ordinary precast concrete benches weather well. Left unpainted, they eventually become mossy and naturally aged; bear in mind that although this can look attractive, it can also reduce the practicality of the seat. If you prefer a slicker look, a coat of paint will do the trick. Metal designs are also suitable, especially hardy aluminum, which will not rust. Plastic tables and chairs may be left outside, but constant exposure to the elements does make many types brittle and they invariably deteriorate over a period of time.

PLANTING

As the ultimate finishing touch for paths, steps, and patios, plants can make all the difference. Flowering creepers and climbers will introduce color on the patio, while hardy ground cover and small perennials will add interest to paths, steps, and paving.

There are numerous ways in which to introduce plants. You may want to establish flowerbeds along the edge of a patio, build planters, or perhaps leave out sections of the paving and plant small shrubs in the spaces. Paths and steps may be flanked with shrubs, or you might consider sprinkling seed on paving laid without mortar and allowing the plants to grow in a spontaneous fashion.

Plants alternating with hard surfaces (see page 24) can be attractive, and this approach may be adapted to paths, steps, and patios alike. Sweet-smelling ground cover like creeping thyme and pennyroyal are good choices.

Whatever the plan, it is essential to do a little homework before you plant and to make sure that the plants you choose will thrive in the environment in which you want to plant them. You will not always be able to imitate a look (perhaps seen in a book or magazine) with exactly the same plants. However, it is usually possible to find a species which may be substituted. Remember that in most parts of the U.S., ground cover will need frequent watering.

A precast concrete seat on an informal patio invites one to stop awhile.

A concrete lantern introduces a touch of oriental style.

Bricks are a versatile material for building paths, steps and patios.

Concrete steps are coloured with pigment to enhance their appearance.

All building projects, no matter how simple, require a selection of tools and materials, as well as a fundamental knowledge of the basic construction principles involved. If you have undertaken construction projects previously, you probably already have most or all of the necessary equipment in your tool kit, and you should be accustomed to much of the terminology used by builders. If not, it is essential to familiarize yourself with the basics and to ensure that you have all the items required before starting work.

MATERIALS

A fairly wide range of materials are suitable for the construction of paths, steps, and patios, and many of these materials are discussed on pages 20-25. A number of them are simply laid on the ground or on a base of soft sand, while others, including bricks, blocks, concrete and lumber (if used for steps) demand some construction skills (see pages 35-39).

Bricks and blocks

Bricks and blocks are available in a vast range, and all may be used to build paths, steps, and patios. Clay, concrete, and calcium silicate bricks and blocks are all perfectly suitable for the construction of steps and patio walls, while special pavers (which are made of clay or precast concrete in a range of colors) are often preferred for patios and pathways.

While there is a huge variety of block sizes, bricks are usually standard in size, ranging from about 9 inches long by 4 inches wide, and about 3 inches thick, depending on where they are made. Facebricks, which are not meant to be rendered, are generally slightly thicker than stock bricks, which are usually rendered with mortar (see page 30.) Paving bricks, which normally have a lightly textured surface, are considerably thinner, and can be as little as $1^{3}/_{4}$ thick.

In addition to flat-sided pavers, concrete units are sometimes molded into shapes which enable them to interlock. These are particularly suitable for driveways which will take reasonably heavy traffic or which are built on a slope.

In spite of minor differences in size, you can estimate quantities for building or paving based on the assumption that you will need 920 bricks or pavers to lay 10 x 20 feet of paving, 45-50 bricks to lay 3 square feet of half-brick walling (one brick-width thick), and 100 to lay 3 square feet of single-brick walling (two brick-widths or 8 inches thick).

Concrete and mortar

Both precast concrete and concrete cast *in situ* are immensely useful for the construction of paths, steps, and patios. Concrete is also used on occasion to form the base slab for patios, particularly if they are to be tiled or topped with materials such as fieldstone, slate, or marble.

Mortar is used extensively for laying brick steps, and for any stairway or patio walls, as well as for some types of paving. It is also used for screeding concrete slabs that are to be topped with tiles, as well as for rendering some brick and block structures, including steps.

Reconstituted stone flags and precast concrete slabs are popular and practical options for patio floors. These materials are cast in the factory to a variety of specifications, and as they are simple to lay, they are particularly suitable for the amateur builder.

Interlocking blocks for terraces and retaining walls are a less usual but nonetheless versatile option for building steps. They are manufactured in a range of designs, although availability varies from place to place. The shape of each unit will also determine how it is used. Some types must be laid with the open surface uppermost, which means you will need to fill the block with dirt or, preferably, concrete to create a level tread. Alternatively you may top the finished step with a precast tile or slab, or perhaps a simulated railroad tie (see pages 42-45. It may be possible to lay modular units on their sides, creating a smooth, solid tread. If this is possible, it is wise to shovel mortar or soil into the hollow, central section of each one.

Concrete cast *in situ* is one of the most widely used materials for both paths and driveways. It is also a popular option for steps, and an

Precast concrete slabs are easy to lay and make great paths.

Interlocking terrace blocks are perfect for steps.

Circular concrete slabs with attractive planting.

Timber poles are used for risers and stringers, the treads are still to be filled with gravel.

essential material for patios that require a solid sub-base. Made by combining cement, sand, and crushed stone (or coarse gravel) with water, it is a versatile and economical material, but one which takes considerable time and effort to mix and lay.

There are several possibilities when it comes to purchasing concrete. You can buy the dry materials in bags, premixed and ready to be combined with water, or separately for mixing by hand or in a concrete mixer, or you can arrange to have it delivered ready for use. Ready-mixed concrete is only a feasible option if a large volume is required, and the premixed dry materials are not economical unless very small quantities are called for. For this reason, most amateur builders opt to buy all the necessary constituents individually and to mix them themselves.

You will need to use a concrete mix suitable for the project you plan to tackle. This will depend partly on the nature of the project, as well as on local conditions and the quality of the materials used. For instance, a 1:3:6 cement: sand: stone mix is suitable for most garden foundations, provided a relatively fine, well-graded aggregate is available. However, the crushed stone

sold in many places will result in concrete which is too stony, and in this instance, a 1:4:4 mixture is preferred. For paths, steps, and exposed slabs, it is best to use a 1:2:3 or 1:3:3 mix.

If concrete is ordered ready-mixed, you will need to give the suppliers details of your project so that they can determine the required strength of the concrete and thus the kind of mix they will need to prepare for you.

Mortar, made by mixing cement and sand with water, is used to bond bricks or blocks and give the structure, paved

surface or edging maximum strength.

Just as cement, sand, and crushed stone are mixed in different ratios for concrete, so too are the cement and sand used for mortar mixes. Generally, it is acceptable to use a 1:4 or even a 1:5 mortar mix for brickwork or paving with clay bricks. If concrete bricks or blocks are used, it is best to make up a weaker 1:6 mixture which is consistent with the building units used.

Cement is a very fine gray powder used to make both concrete and mortar, and as such is one of the most important ingredients in just about every building project. Several types are suitable, but ordinary Portland cement is most popular. It is sold in 100-pound bags (and sometimes 50 pounds and 75 pounds.)

Cement hardens when it is mixed with water, and it is this chemical reaction which gives concrete and mortar their strength. It is worth remembering that cement will not gain full strength if it dries out too quickly, so concrete and mortar should be kept damp while they set and cure.

Bear in mind, too, that unless cement is stored away from moisture, it is likely to form lumps and become unusable. Stack it in a dry place above the ground, and use it within two to three months. Discard any cement that has become lumpy or hard.

The quantity of cement needed for any project will, of course, depend on

Freestanding edgings must always be laid on mortar.

A patio being screeded with mortar before it is tiled.

the strength of the mixture required. When using a 1:4:4 ratio, you can base estimates on 5 x 100 pound bags of cement being enough for 3 cubic feet of concrete; for a 1:3:6 mix, you will need four bags, six for a 1:3:3 mix and eight if the ratio is 1:2:3.

Sand is an important ingredient in mortar, both for bricklaying and for rendering brick and block surfaces, and it is invaluable as a bedding material beneath all types of paving. Furthermore, the properties of the sand used to make concrete will have a marked effect on the final product.

The best building sands are evenly graded with particles of various sizes, no bigger than 2 inches, and with 4-5% of the sand consisting of very fine material, sometimes referred to as fines. Poorly graded sand will produce concrete which is difficult to work with, while a lack of fines will result in a mixture which is hard to compact properly.

While the source of the sand you are using is not necessarily a reliable guide to its quality, it is worth knowing that natural river sand is generally clean and free of clay, and pit sands are usually well graded. Crusher sand, manufactured for building purposes from crushed rocks, should be of a suitable quality for concrete work, but crusher dust is too fine. Beach sand contains shell particles and salt, and unless it has been professionally washed, should not be used. Mine-dump sand and fine, wind-blown sand from desert areas should be avoided.

In addition, the sand used for making concrete should be reasonably coarse ("sharp"), while that used for mortar and plaster should be softer, with more fines. When flexible paving is laid (see page 39), the sand used beneath the bricks should be coarser than that used to joint them. Coarse river sand is suitable.

In some areas, suppliers add lime to sand and sell it as "plaster sand" (as it is used to make mortar for plastering or rendering brickwork), "mortar mix," or "lime sand." In this case, additional lime is not required (see below).

Sand is sold in 100-pound (or sometimes 75 pounds) by builders' suppliers and most hardware stores. If you want a large volume, it is best to order in bulk. The smallest quantity most merchants will deliver is half a cubic yard. Sand delivered in bulk will be dumped outside your house. If you live in a windy area, cover it as soon as possible with plastic sheeting to prevent it from being blown away.

Stone, the coarse aggregate in concrete, is screened to size specially for construction purposes. In some areas natural pebbles and pea gravel are available, otherwise you will have to use crushed stone, supplied in "single sizes." For home improvement purposes, $\frac{1}{2}$ inch or $\frac{1}{4}$ inch stone is best. The smallest size commonly available is $\frac{1}{16}$ inch . While it is true that the smaller the stone, the easier it is to work with the concrete, you will need more cement for the concrete to gain the same strength, and this will also make it more costly. All quantities recommended here assume that you are using $\frac{1}{2}$ inch stone.

Like sand, crushed stone is usually available from builders' suppliers and hardware stores that the appropriate tools and materials. Alternatively, this material may also be delivered in bulk. Your choice will depend on what sort of quantity you require.

Lime is a useful ingredient which makes mortar more workable and aids water retention, and should always be included in the mix if the sand lacks sufficient very fine particles. Since it improves the plasticity and cohesiveness of the mortar, the addition of lime will make it easier to render a surface and will improve bonding between bricks and mortar. It will also help to prevent the rendered (or plastered) surface from cracking.

Available in 50-pound sacks from builders' suppliers, hydrated builders' lime should not be confused with agricultural lime, road lime, or quicklime (calcium oxide), all of which should be avoided.

Plasticizer is a popular alternative to lime in some areas. Normally sold in a minimum of 5 quarts, it is mixed with the mortar according to the manufacturer's instructions – usually 1 fl. ounce to every 100 pounds cement.

Lumber

Lumber used to build pergolas and patio seating, decks, and wooden steps, should be durable and structurally sound. Although you will be governed by what is available in your area, ensure that the lumber has been treated and will withstand weathering.

While poles can be used to build rustic pergolas, sawn and planed timber is more commonly chosen for decks and steps. Both softwoods (from coniferous trees) and hardwoods (from broadleafed species) may be used, although some types will be more suitable than others, and some species more expensive. Wood is

A rustic approach with logs.

graded according to its strength and appearance. Buying the best quality you can afford always pays off. If possible, avoid lumber that bows or twists. Also be careful of splitting, and of large knots which may cause the timber to break.

Railroad ties and sliced logs are both useful for pathways. Since any type of lumber will tend to become slippery in wet weather, it is usually sensible to alternate the pieces of wood with other materials, or to plant ground cover plants in between them.

TOOLS

The basic tool kit required to construct a patio, path, or simple garden stairway is within the means of most people. Although some power tools, for instance a drill and a saw, will make carpentry easier, most projects can be completed with hand-tools. Larger items, including concrete mixers and compacting machines (which are useful for the more ambitious paving job) can be rented.

General items

Virtually every project you tackle will require a spade and perhaps a shovel, a hammer, wheelbarrow, and tape measure. Without these basic tools you will not be able to set out the area accurately or excavate it.

Tape measures are probably the first item in any tool kit. You will need a good quality retractable steel tape, ideally with a locking mechanism which makes it easier to handle if you are working single-handed. They come in various lengths, 25 feet and 50 feet are both useful.

Pegs and line are used to set out paths, steps, and patios. Although you can use genuine builders' line (commonly used to ensure that brick courses are straight during bricklaying), ordinary string will suffice. Make the pegs from excess or reject lumber or offcuts.

Chalk is sold for setting out building sites, but it can be expensive. Instead you can use powdered cement or even flour, a much less expensive solution.

Spades and shovels are indispensable for all projects. You will need a spade to dig foundations and to prepare the sub-base for patios, as well as to level paths and excavate steps. A shovel, which has a slightly rounded shape (with either a curved or squared-off end), is better suited for shifting loose material as well as for mixing concrete and mortar.

Picks or mattocks are useful if you are excavating hard ground or removing large stones and rocks.

Wheelbarrows are essential for transporting materials on site and useful for mixing small quantities of concrete and mortar. Invest in a builder's wheelbarrow, preferably with a pneumatic tire, gardening wheelbarrows are not suitable for building work.

Hammers are the handyman's best friend. Officially part of the carpenter's toolkit, they are also used for knocking in pegs, extracting nails, and assembling forms for concreting and profiles for steps. In addition to an ordinary claw hammer, you will find that a hefty club hammer is useful for heavy-duty tasks (knocking in pegs or forms). A brick hammer (which has a chisel end instead of a claw) is the answer when it comes to breaking

Timber is a versatile material in the garden.

A builder's square is essential for accuracy.

A spade is an indispensable tool.

bricks for bricklaying and paving, and a rubber mallet (essentially a hammer with a heavy, rubber-topped head) is invaluable for knocking paving bricks, blocks, and slabs into place.

Tools for leveling and checking

Good building practice demands that brickwork is level and plumb, that paved surfaces are flat and that the corners of all structures or paving are square or set accurately at the correct angle. Certain inexpensive tools will help to ensure accuracy; some of them may even be made at home.

Spirit levels are used to check that both vertical and horizontal surfaces are level, no matter what materials you are using. Available in several lengths, they usually incorporate two spirit vials. If the bubble in the vial is centered, the surface is level. Although 4 feet is a handy length, you will have to use it in conjunction with a straight-edged piece of wood if you are checking a patio or a long path. Alternatively, work with a line level, which comprises a vial indicator attached to a length of builder's line.

Water levels are simple home-made tools which work well over large areas and are invaluable when you are setting out a slope or when there is a need to establish points at the same height around a corner. They are also a useful aid in making a profile for steps

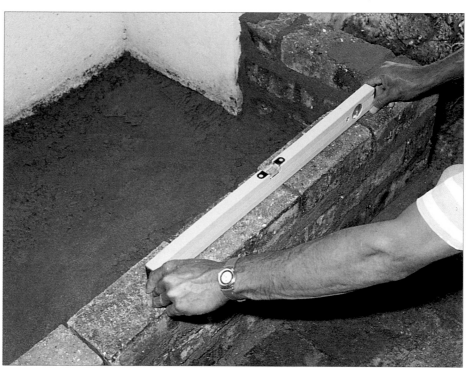

A spirit level must be used throughout the building project.

(see page 40.) All you need is a length of transparent tubing (or a hosepipe with a length of transparent tubing inserted at each end) filled with water. Working on the principle that water finds its own level, attach one end to a post or to brickwork so that the water is at a specific height (the datum level), then take the other end of the tube to another point whose height you wish to measure, taking care not to spill any. The level of the water here will

be exactly the same height.

Squares are vital for checking right angles. Steel builder's squares are fairly bulky tools, but more accurate than a home-made square made from sawn timber assembled to form a right-angled triangle. They are usually marked off in customary and/or metric measurements. Smaller combination squares (also used for carpentry) incorporate a spirit vial and are useful when you are working on a small

A wooden float is used to smooth mortar.

A wooden pole may be used for compacting.

scale, for example if you want to check that timber steps are square. Of course, you can use a home-made square to lay out a patio; to make one, cut three lengths of sawn wood in the ratio 3:4:5 (for instance 3 feet, 4 feet and 5 feet) and join them to form a triangle. Alternatively, use the 3:4:5 method, measuring and pegging to check for square (see page 35).

Tools for construction

When it comes to building, whether you are going to tackle bricklaying, concretework, or paving, there are certain tools which you cannot be without. Others will merely simplify the task at hand.

Compactors are needed to flatten the sub-base for paving, to compress the backfill behind steps and in some cases to compact paving once it has been laid. While a mechanical vibrator (which may be hired for the project) is essential if there is fill (broken bricks, stones, and so on) beneath a patio, it is usually sufficient to use a home-made punner or ramming tool. For small projects, even a thick pole will suffice. To make your own punner, set a post of some sort (a broom handle is fine) in an empty 5-quart paint can and fill the can with concrete. Alternatively, weld a metal plate to a metal pole or fix a heavy block of wood to a post.

If a mechanical plate vibrator is used to level paving, care should be taken to avoid damage – a single pass of the compactor is usually sufficient, since going over the same area a few times may cause the pavers to crack.

Concrete mixers are useful for jobs which require a large volume of concrete. They can be rented in several sizes, and may be powered by electricity, gasoline, or diesel.

Trowels, used for bricklaying, rendering brick and block surfaces, and flattening small areas of concrete, are available in different shapes and sizes. The kind you use will depend upon the application.

Mortarboards and screedboards are used by professional bricklayers to hold small quantities of mortar while they work. These are useful but not essential tools.

Floats, made from both wood and metal, are used to smooth the mortar used for rendering and for screeds laid over concrete.

Woodworking tools

These are necessary for constructing decks, timber steps, and pergolas, and include drills (see below), hammers, and a variety of saws and screwdrivers. Since both the forms for *in situ* concrete and the profiles for steps are commonly made from wood, it

is a good idea to include at least one of each in your toolkit. A good range of handsaws is easy to find. Useful saws include the general-purpose bowsaw, which is ideal for sawing logs, the sturdy cabinet saw, with a rectangular blade, which is best for cutting smaller sections of lumber, the larger panel saw, and the hacksaw, which will cut through just about anything, including metal. You probably have screwdrivers already, but if not, consider investing in a spiral ratchet screwdriver which, with its variable positions and reverse action, not only simplifies the task of screwing in fasteners, but also allows you to remove them relatively easily.

Power tools

Although not an essential requirement for the average path, patio, or step project, several power tools can make life easier. An electric saw, in particular, will enable you to cut timber with little effort, while a drill will simplify the insertion of bolts and screws. An angle grinder is invaluable for cutting thick tiles and bricks, while a block splitter or masonry saw is indispensable for cutting any precast concrete products.

Larger power tools, such as concrete mixers, compactors, and vibrators, can usually be hired for a particular building project if necessary.

PRINCIPLES & TECHNIQUES

You will need only rudimentary skills to build straightforward steps or to lay an ordinary path or patio, but it is vital to have a thorough understanding of the principles which support good building practice. You will also have to master certain basic techniques if you plan to undertake the work yourself.

The basics

The one essential rule is to keep everything you construct square, level, and plumb. This means that bricks and blocks must be laid in straight lines or at right angles to one another, and their upper surface should be flat, while paving must be smooth and even. If you ignore the rules, walls, however low, may fall over and water will accumulate in uneven paving and on the treads of steps.

Square structures and paved areas have right-angled corners, so unless a patio is irregular in form, you will need to ensure that each corner measures exactly 90°. Although paths frequently curve, most steps are also "square," that is, the treads and risers have right-angled corners and the steps are parallel to each other.

When setting out a square design, the simplest way to check that all corners are at right angles is to use the 3:4:5 method (unless you use a builder's square or make a square with timber – see page 34). Mark out the patio and then measure 9 feet from the corner along one side, and 12 feet from the same corner along the

adjacent side. Then measure the distance between the two points. If it is exactly 15 feet, your patio is square; if not, adjust the layout until the sides of the structure measure 9 feet, 12 feet and 15 feet. If your patio is less than 12 feet long, or if you are checking for square in a confined space, simply use smaller measurements which are multiples of three, four and five (6 feet, 8 feet and 110 feet, for instance).

Circular areas are not difficult to lay out – you will simply need to make yourself a large compass with pegs and a length of string. Knock one peg in at a central point, attach the string to it, then pull the string taut. Mark the string with the desired radius, then use it to find several points on the circumference, and mark them with pegs. Join up the points with a chalk or flour line.

Level and plumb are terms every builder is familiar with. The tools used to ensure that these principles are followed are detailed on pages 33-34, but the one you will use most often is a spirit level. This is used to check all horizontal surfaces (brick paving, slabs, and the treads of steps) as well as vertical surfaces. Although all your upright surfaces, including patio walls

and the risers of steps, must be exactly vertical, paved areas and the treads of steps will usually slope very slightly to aid drainage (see below). If you are considering laying a ramp instead of steps, bear in mind that the gradient should not exceed 1:5 for a normal ramp or 1:12 for wheelchair access.

Drainage

Water is the life-blood of any garden, yet it can also undermine foundations and the entire landscaping framework, washing away plants and paving, and causing substantial damage at times. Even if the soil is stable and the ground absolutely level, patios and paths must be constructed so that excess rainwater drains away from buildings and does not accumulate in pools on the surface.

Subsurface drainage must not be overlooked. Regardless of the materials used, the durability of garden paving and the structures that go with it will depend to a large extent on the stability of the ground beneath it. If the site is level and the soil drains naturally, you can lay most materials on a bed of sand without any additional subsurface drainage. If, however, there is a high clay content or swampy areas are evident in fine weather, it is advisable to lay a sub-base of

An angle grinder cuts bricks quickly.

A circular paving pattern is an attractive option.

well-compacted hardcore or crushed stone under the surface. Perforated plastic pipe buried in this sub-base will help to draw off water to a surface channel or a soakaway. Alternatively, porous geosynthetic pipes (made from high-density polyethylene) wrapped in filter fabric (permeable polyester geotextiles) may be used. These may also be set in narrow trenches along the edges of paths,

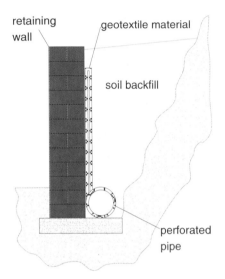

retaining wall

geotextile material

soil backfill

perforated pipe

A fin drain behind a retaining wall.

driveways, patios, and so on to create a very effective drainage system.

On sloping properties or where substantial drainage is necessary (behind a retaining wall, for instance,) a vertical drain may be required. The most common type is made by setting pipework into a French drain filled with rubble and stone. This can involve substantial earthworks, but instead, a prefabricated fin drain may be installed if the materials are available. Lightweight and simple to install, this kind of drain is made by wrapping geotextile material (kept rigid by a layer of synthetic geonet) around geosynthetic pipework (see above), so that the fabric extends above the pipe to form a fin. Water is attracted to the highly absorbent fin, and flows down to the pipe, which directs it away from the base of the slope. It is ideal for the owner-builder to install as it obviates the need for cumbersome hardcore and stone, and cuts down on both transport and labor costs.

Some form of drainage will also be needed behind most steps, unless they are very gradual and located away from buildings and paved areas.

In most instances it is sufficient simply to backfill behind each riser with well-compacted crushed stone or gravel. If the steps are steep or involve a retaining wall, it may also be necessary to lead a pipe from a drain behind the structure to divert the water, or to use a fin drain.

Surface drainage is necessary to channel water away from buildings, and there should be a fall of about 1:40 or 1:50 across any patio, path, driveway, or other paved area. With practice, you will soon learn to judge just how off-center the bubble in the spirit-level vial should be to achieve this run-off. To establish the correct gradient, attach a small block of wood under one end of a 2x4 and place the spirit level on top; the bubble in the vial should be exactly centered. To achieve a gradient of 1:40, use a 1-inch block under a 3-foot long 2x4; for 1:50, use a ³/₄-inch block. It is also good building practice to set up a line as a guide following the angle of the 2x4. The finished surface of the patio should be below the inside floor level, and if there is a damp-proof course in the walls, the patio floor should be at least 6 inches below the top of it. In cases where the interior floors are made of wood, the upper surface of paving, concrete, and so on should be below the bottom of the floorboards.

If you want to divert rainwater underground, you will have to build a gully or lay a precast channel above the ground, and direct this into a subsurface drainage system. You will not usually be permitted to drain surface water into an existing sewerage system, but you may be able to link up with a storm drain.

Often, drainage is not an issue with garden paths. However, solid pathways (including those which are brick-paved or made from concrete laid *in situ*) should be fractionally lower on one side than the other to allow for a run-off, while the treads of steps should slope down to the front very slightly (no more than 1:100) to prevent the formation of pools of water and puddles and help drain away flash floodwater quickly.

It is essential to allow for drainage on all sites.

Pebbles are used to camouflage a rainwater drainage channel .

A concrete mixer simplifies the task.

Concreting

Working with concrete can be arduous, but the principles involved are not complicated. It is important to ensure that the proportions of cement, sand, and crushed stone are correct and that you mix it properly with just the right quantity of water. Certain guidelines should also be followed when laying the concrete.

The proportions of cement, sand, and stone (aggregate) used for concretework depend primarily on the use to which the concrete will be put. Generally there are three grades of concrete – low strength, medium strength, and high strength – although the actual ratios of the dry materials used will sometimes vary depending on the quality of the materials available (see page 30). While low-strength concrete is commonly used for foundations and footings, a medium strength is preferred for garden footpaths, domestic driveways, and steps, and for patio slabs that will be exposed to weathering. High-strength concrete is really only necessary for watertight walls and industrial situations, or driveways that will take very heavy traffic.

Mixing concrete is a laborious task. Even if you have a mechanical concrete mixer (see page 34), you will have to shovel the dry materials into the machine. Whether you are mixing by hand or by machine, you will also have to measure the materials in batches to ensure that the proportions used are accurate. Those recommended on page 31 specify quantities by volume, so use one strong, rigid container (a builder's bucket or a clean 25 quart paint can) for measuring.

If you have a machine, load the stone with a little water first to prevent the mortar from building up on the blades, then load the sand, and finally the cement and more water. When mixing by hand, combine the cement and sand first, either in a wheelbarrow or on a flat, dry surface. Do not mix them directly on the ground as soil, dead leaves, and small twigs will almost inevitably get mixed in, and water may be absorbed from the mixture. Make a crater in the center, then add water, shovelling the dry mixture from the edges to the center. Once it is smooth, add the stone and continue shoveling. Aim for a firm, consistent mixture which is neither too liquid nor too dry.

Formwork (shuttering) is essential if concrete is to be laid above ground level or if steps are to be built from concrete cast *in situ*. Various materials are suitable for this framework, including lumber. Old 2x4s may be used, provided they have reasonably straight edges and are rigid enough to bear the weight of the amount of concrete to be poured. For a curved path, you will need formwork which can be bent to shape. Hardboard (masonite) is ideal as it is reasonably flexible but strong enough to support the concrete. You will need to hold the

Stone steps laid on a concrete foundation alongside a concrete pond.

Creative use of bricks and crazy paving in an attractive courtyard.

chopping movement. As water comes to the surface, use a smoother sawing motion to level the concrete to the height of the formwork. Make sure there are no gaps or hollows.

If you are planning to screed the surface of the concrete with mortar (for tiles, perhaps), the finish of your slab will not be important, but if the concrete itself forms the surface of the patio, path, or treads of steps, you will want an even finish. Use a wooden float to smooth it or a stiff-bristled broom to create a rough texture. Alternatively, for a slip-proof finish, scatter fine crushed stone or pebbles on the wet surface and tamp lightly with a float or straightedge. When the concrete has almost set, spray with water and brush with a stiff broom to expose the aggregate.

When laying concrete over a fairly large area, you will need to create expansion joints to help prevent cracking. Do this by working in sections no larger than 10 x 10 feet, and laying alternate panels. When the first panels have set, fill the remaining areas between them with more concrete.

Allow the concrete to set thoroughly before you remove any shuttering. Do not allow it to dry out too rapidly or it may well crack. In hot weather, cover it with burlap or plastic sheeting, or moisten it now and then with water.

Brickwork and paving

Laying paving and building with bricks or blocks are skills which are easily mastered, but before you start to lay bricks, be sure that you can use a trowel correctly. Wherever you work with mortar, you will need this tool to butter the ends of bricks, and to make sure that they are laid evenly. Having done this, you will simply need to follow the basic principles and ensure that your work is square, level, and plumb (see page 35).

Mortar is a material used in all bricklaying and some types of paving. Made from cement, sand and, in some instances lime (see pages 30-31,) it is mixed in the same way as concrete. First combine the dry materials on a clean, flat surface or in a wheelbarrow,

shuttering in place with loose pegs, or nail it to flat stakes which can be hammered into the ground (see pages 46-48.) Whichever method is used, make sure that the pegs or stakes are on the outside of the formwork.

Laying or pouring concrete is much easier if you have help. Before you start, wet the ground to prevent the moisture in the concrete from being absorbed into the ground and possibly causing cracking. Either shovel the mixture into the trench or formwork, or pour it directly from the wheelbarrow. Chop into the concrete with your spade to allow trapped air to escape, and compact it roughly with the back of the spade or shovel. Then use a straight-edged 2x4 to compact the concrete more thoroughly, using a then add water to them. Aim for a mixture which is thick and smooth but not watery, and only mix as much as you can use in a couple of hours. If the mortar gets hard, discard it because adding water will weaken the mixture.

Bricklaying is one of those skills which improve with practice. The more bricks you lay, the easier it becomes. Whatever you are building, the techniques are exactly the same.

The first course of all walls (including the risers of steps) and most edgings around patios are bedded in wet mortar. Start by laying a long strip of the mixture along the line where the bricks are to be laid. Use a bricklayer's trowel to create a furrow through the middle of the mortar, and place the first brick in position. The end of the next and subsequent bricks may be buttered, or you can use a trowel to fill in the gaps (which should be about 1/8 inch thick) once the bricks are in place on the bed of mortar. Use a spirit level to make sure that the first course is level. If bricks are not properly aligned, tap them firmly with the handle of the trowel. If necessary, lift the bricks and add or remove mortar.

The next course is laid in the same way, with a 1/8-inch wide joint and mortar separating the bricks. Stringing a builder's line along each course will help to keep the wall straight. You can keep the line in place with metal pegs, or wrap a builders' line around a pair of corner blocks (L-shaped blocks of wood with a slot and groove cut in each to accommodate the string,) and hook the blocks onto the corners of the brick-work with the builders' line pulled taut.

An essential principle of good brickwork is bonding. If a wall or riser is laid so that the bricks don't bond and form a solid mass with an evenly distributed load, it will lack strength and stability. There are several different types, the most common being stretcher bond, where each brick overlaps the two below it by half.

Paving must always be laid so that the water drains off it effectively. This means that you should aim for an even slope with a gradient of no more than 1:40 (see page 36.) You may need to include some type of edging restraint.

The material chosen for your paved surface will largely determine how it is laid. The basic choice is between setting slabs, bricks, or blocks on a bed of sand and setting them in mortar. Bricks may be laid in any number of patterns, some of which bond particularly well and are therefore popular for driveways and surfaces intended for heavy foot traffic. A running bond (the horizontal equivalent of stretcher bond) is fairly common, as are both basketweave and herring-bone patterns.

The simplest and least expensive form of brick paving is laid on sand. Known as flexible paving, it requires no mortar except for the edging, and sand is brushed into the joints. However, bricks can be laid on sand and brushed either with a very weak mixture of dry cement and sand or a crumbly, moist mixture between the joints, then sprayed with water.

Rigid paving is more time-consuming, and because mortar is required it is also more costly. However, this method is preferred for steps, as it is more stable. There are various methods of laying rigid paving, all involving setting the bricks on a mortar bed. You can either butter the ends of the bricks as you lay them in place, or fill the joints later by brushing a dry cement and sand mix over them, and then spraying the entire surface with water.

An unconventional bond pattern used for a path.

Herringbone pattern.

Basketweave pattern.

Running bond.

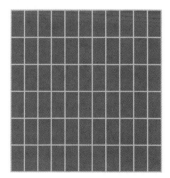
Stack bond or jack-on-jack.

STEP-BY-STEP BUILDING METHODS

Once you have a good understanding of the building principles involved and a thorough knowledge of the materials available and the tools to be used, you can get down to work. The step-by-step instructions which follow will guide you through several different building methods suitable for a range of paths, steps, and patios. Once you have mastered these, you should be well equipped to tackle any of the projects on pages 54-63, or to create and produce a design of your own without any formal assistance.

The first building method shown here uses lumber and will enable you to construct a simple flight of steps. You will need only a few tools and very basic carpentry skills.

A path, patio, and steps built from a range of precast concrete materials, may be adapted for virtually any loose-laid paving material, such as cut logs, stepping-stones, railroad ties, and any other precast units. Here, the steps are built from modular blocks that are normally used to build retaining walls, while the path and patio are laid out with a combination of materials, all made from precast concrete. The 3:4:5 method of checking right-angled corners (see page 35) is shown in action, and the importance of keeping horizontal surfaces exactly level is clearly illustrated.

The principles of concretework are shown in detail in the step-by-step photographs, which follow through construction of steps and a pathway built from concrete cast *in situ*. Both straight and curved formwork (shuttering) are shown to illustrate how versatile this much-maligned building material really is. The same method may be followed by anyone wishing to build a concrete patio slab.

The dimensions and the quantities of materials would vary and you will also have to lay out the area as shown in the step-by-step section on precast materials (pages 42-45).

Basic paving skills are illustrated in two step-by-step sections which show two methods of laying brick paving, as well as two different types of step. These may, of course, be combined in any way to suit your needs.

On pages 50 and 51 a brick patio and path are built on a bed of sand and a mixture of cement and sand is brushed into the joints; the steps shown here are built into a slope. On pages 52 and 53, the paving is laid on sand over a concrete slab, and the joints are filled with sand. The steps in this project are built up from the flat surface of the patio, linking this outside area with the house.

PLANNING STEPS

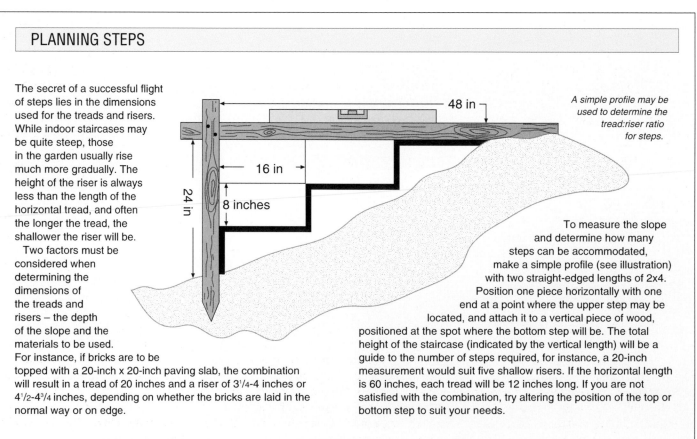

The secret of a successful flight of steps lies in the dimensions used for the treads and risers. While indoor staircases may be quite steep, those in the garden usually rise much more gradually. The height of the riser is always less than the length of the horizontal tread, and often the longer the tread, the shallower the riser will be.

Two factors must be considered when determining the dimensions of the treads and risers – the depth of the slope and the materials to be used. For instance, if bricks are to be topped with a 20-inch x 20-inch paving slab, the combination will result in a tread of 20 inches and a riser of 3¼-4 inches or 4½-4¾ inches, depending on whether the bricks are laid in the normal way or on edge.

A simple profile may be used to determine the tread:riser ratio for steps.

To measure the slope and determine how many steps can be accommodated, make a simple profile (see illustration) with two straight-edged lengths of 2x4. Position one piece horizontally with one end at a point where the upper step may be located, and attach it to a vertical piece of wood, positioned at the spot where the bottom step will be. The total height of the staircase (indicated by the vertical length) will be a guide to the number of steps required, for instance, a 20-inch measurement would suit five shallow risers. If the horizontal length is 60 inches, each tread will be 12 inches long. If you are not satisfied with the combination, try altering the position of the top or bottom step to suit your needs.

Wooden steps are useful not only for decks built above ground level, but also for spanning slopes in the garden and for providing access to places that are otherwise hard to reach.

There are many ways to build steps from wood. This project illustrates a very simple approach, with open risers.

If the steps lead to a porch, stoop, or a raised patio, you will need to attach a ledger or wall-plate to the wall to support the stringers (the strips of wood on either side of the flight of steps).

MATERIALS

Any lumber suitable for outdoor construction may be used for these steps. It must be sturdy enough to take the weight of people using it, and should be pretreated with a suitable preservative. Most types are pressure-treated in the factory and will only need to be coated with a sealant of some sort for protection from the weather, if possible before assembling the steps.

Softwood planks which measure 9 x 1 1/2 inches are used for the treads and the stringers, while 1 1/2 x 1 1/2-inch battens are used for the cleats which support the treads.

To prevent rust, only galvanized or brass fasteners should be used. In this instance, 3 1/4-inch galvanized coach screws and 3 3/4-inch long 1 3/4-inch countersunk brass screws.

The two stringers are set in concrete for stability. Presuming you are using a 1:4:4 mix, you will need 120 pounds of cement and 495 pounds each of sand and 1/4-inch crushed stone.

1 Determine the dimensions of the steps (see page 40), then cut the planks to size with an electric circular saw or a hand-saw. Cut one end of each cleat off at an angle for a neater finish, ensuring that they are shorter than the stringers are wide.

2 You will also need to cut the ends of the stringers at an angle so that they can abut the deck fascia or ledger neatly. Paint the ends that are to be buried in the ground with bitumen or creosote to protect the wood from moisture and termites.

3 Attach the cleats to the stringers at equal intervals (depending on the height and number of steps to be constructed), using a combination square to position them. Drill through both pieces of wood at either end of the cleats, then screw them together firmly.

4 Mark the position of the bottom step and dig a 8-inch x 12-inch footing, 8 inches deep, for each stringer. Position the two stringers and bolt them to the deck or ledger. Alternatively, secure them with angle brackets and suitable screws.

5 Brace the stringers securely, using battens or other timber offcuts, and check that they are correctly aligned. Mix the concrete and fill the two holes, compacting it with the back of a spade or shovel. Allow to set overnight before proceeding.

6 The last step is to fix the planks to the cleats to form treads. Make sure that they are level, then drill through the upper surface of each tread into the supporting cleat. Screw the two together, then fill all holes with a suitable wood filler.

Some of the prettiest paths, steps, and patios are constructed using widely available precast concrete products, such as slabs, fake flagstones, and imitation ties. There is a huge variety, and if the type shown here is not available in your location, substitute something similar, or adapt the design to suit your needs.

Irrespective of what you decide to use, preparation of the site will be exactly the same. Essentially, you will need to ensure that there is a solid sub-base, and then lay the slabs on a bed of sand. A certain amount of excavation may be necessary, and in some cases (particularly where the soil does not drain well) a layer of hardcore will have to be laid beneath an area to be paved.

The shape of your site will determine whether you build the steps, path, or patio first. In this instance, it was sensible to start with the steps, as this made access up the slope easier during the rest of the building process. Since the path is slightly lower than the patio here, it was laid last. The simplicity of laying precast slabs and blocks on sand makes the entire operation very flexible, and mistakes are easy to rectify.

MATERIALS

Rounded precast concrete blocks, designed for the construction of modular retaining walls, are used to build these steps. In this case, the units are approximately 11 inches wide, 14 inches deep and 8 inches high. Designs vary, but the basic concept of interlocking units remains the same, and any type may be used. Since they are laid with the open side uppermost, the treads are topped with a precast imitation railroadtie, giving the steps a neater and more attractive finish. Another option is to fill the blocks with a relatively weak concrete mix and screed the upper surface with mortar. Alternatively, look for modular terrace blocks which may be laid on their side, but remember that these should be filled with dirt or concrete for stability.

The patio, which has a border of heavy concrete kerbstones, is laid using reconstructed stone paving slabs made in three different sizes, which gives it a random finish and a pleasing, informal look. You could also use old railroad ties or cut lumber as an edging, and cut stone or ordinary precast concrete slabs for the floor. Stone chips are scattered between the slabs, both for effect and to level the patio surface. Otherwise you could plant a ground cover or low-growing, sweet-scented herbs to soften the look, or you may want to scatter flower seeds amongst the chips to add color and charm.

The same pavers are used for the path, alternating with a row of three imitation ties. Small pebbles may be used between the slabs and ties, and in the case of the patio, various low-growing plants are also an option.

1 The first step is to remove any vegetation from the area where the steps are to be located. If the ground is particularly hard or stony, you will need to use a pick to loosen the soil. Also remove any large rocks before you go any further.

2 Each step must be laid on level ground, so you will need to create rough steps in the embankment. Starting from the bottom, excavate an area of about 40 x 40 inches for the three-block-wide step, which will be 33½ inches wide with a 14-inch tread.

3 Although a concrete foundation is not necessary, every step must be laid on well-compacted ground. A home-made punner is an invaluable and effective ramming tool. You can make one by concreting a wooden pole into a can.

4 It is also essential that each block is laid on a flat, even surface. Use a spirit level to check this, and scrape away dirt if necessary. Place the tool on several spots, and draw it across the soil to make sure that the surface is level in all directions.

5 Place the first three blocks on the prepared surface, making sure that they interlock properly. The convex side of each block should fit snugly into the concave side of the next. The flat surface of each unit faces to the front to create a flat riser.

6 Before filling the gap behind the blocks, it is essential to check that they are completely level. A good way to get them level is to place a little dirt in each hollow and then move them about so that any voids gaps are filled and the blocks sit firmly.

7 Do not rely on guesswork – use a spirit level to ensure that the blocks are level. If the bubble is not completely centered, put a little more sand in the hollow and move the block around a little. If it seems too high, remove some of the sand.

8 Now fill the space behind the blocks with sand or dirt. Never backfill with clay, as this will prevent water from draining away effectively. Use a punner to flatten and compact the soil behind the first step thoroughly before preparing for the next one.

9 Follow the instructions given in steps 2-4, ensuring that the compacted ground behind the blocks is on the same level as the upper surface of the blocks. Place the next row of blocks so that the front edge overlaps the back of the first step.

10 Position and level the blocks as before, then fill them with soil or, if you wish, a weak concrete mixture. Fill the gap behind each step with sand or soil and compact each level in the same way until you get to the top of the slope.

11 Lay tiles or precast concrete ties (as shown here) over the tread of each step. These may be loose-laid or set on a little mortar to keep them in place. Plant a hardy ground cover in the soil at the back of the step to fill the gap.

12 Lay out the path from the top of the steps to the patio site. The path is 40 inches wide because of the length of the ties used. Using a steel tape measure, ensure that the edges are parallel along the entire length, marking with chalk or flour.

13 Although this patio has cut-off corners, it is best to set out a full rectangle before laying the edging kerbstones in place. Use the 3:4:5 method (see page 35), measuring 200 inches across the diagonal, to ensure that the corners are square.

14 Prepare the surface of the path and the patio before you begin laying any of the slabs or stones. The amount of soil you excavate will depend on the thickness of the precast slabs as well as on the natural slope of the ground.

15 Make sure that the base is flat and even, with a slight slope for drainage. Use a spirit level across the path to check that you are not removing too much soil. Although the slabs are to be laid on sand, it should not be used to rectify levels.

16 Build the patio before you lay the pathway. First, level the area where the patio is to be built. As the patio is to be raised above the level of the path, it is not necessary to excavate the soil unless it slopes. Throw any excess soil into the center.

17 To avoid unnecessary digging, it may be possible to fill in slightly in places, building up the level of the ground. Since the area of the patio covers more than 30 sq. feet, you will need to set the spirit level on a long 2x4.

18 You will also need to check the level of the sub-base, diagonally across the surface from corner to corner. Place the straightedge and spirit level on bricks to help establish accurately how much dirt must be removed from any particular place.

19 Once you are certain that the entire area is flat and level (or slopes for drainage, if necessary), you can put the edging in place. Hefty precast concrete kerbstones are used here. Use a steel builder's square to ensure that the corners are at 90°.

20 Position all the kerbstones as shown. If the ground is stable, fill the space within the kerbstones with sand or dirt, otherwise first half-fill the area with hardcore of crushed stone and gravel to aid drainage, then top with sand or dirt.

21 The hardcore and all the sand and soil used as fill must be well compacted before the sand bed is laid. You can use a home-made punner, although a mechanical compacting machine is useful for large areas as it takes less time and is more thorough.

22 The finished level of this sub-base should be below the top of the kerbstones, leaving enough room for a 1-2-inch bed of sand and the paving slabs, which in this case are about 2 inches thick. Cover the surface with soft building sand, the rake it.

23 The sand must be level before you start laying the slabs. Hose it lightly to aid compaction, then drag a 2x4 across the sand, smoothing and leveling it. You will also need to check with a spirit level to ensure that the ground really is level.

24 Start laying the slabs from one of the corners, leaving a small gap between each one. There is no particular plan to follow. Simply place them in an attractive pattern, using a good mix of the three sizes at all times. Use a spirit level to check alignment.

25 If you are not happy with the way the pavers are laid, change them now rather than later. When they are all in place, spread sand over the surface and brush it into the gaps with a stiff-bristled broom, then hose down the area lightly to compact the fill.

26 Spread pebbles or stone chips over the surface, then brush them into the gaps over the sand. Once the stones have settled, you can add more if and where you think it is needed, or you can sow seeds among the stones for an informal effect.

27 The path is laid in much the same way as the patio, but without an edging. Leave space for a step between the kerbstones and where you are to lay the first sleeper. Spread sand along the excavated path, smoothing it out with a spirit level.

28 Position the imitation sleepers across the path, about 2¹⁄₄ inches inches apart. They are usually slightly irregular in thickness, as are wooden ties, and it is sometimes hard to get the upper surface flat. Remove a little of the sand bed if necessary.

29 Leave a gap of 5-6 inches, depending on the curve of the path, and then lay a group of pavers. All the gaps may be planted once the pathway is complete. As plants become established, they will soften the path and give it a pretty, countrified look.

30 Continue laying sets of ties and slabs alternately, until the path is complete. Then build up the step to the patio. Having left a natural step, all you need do now is spread a layer of sand over the slightly elevated surface and level it before laying the ties.

31 Lay two ties close together to form a step up to the patio. If they are slightly unstable, insert three pegs at the front of the two ties to hold them securely in place, knocking them in so that they do not protrude above the upper surface of the step.

Concrete cast *in situ* is an economical and extremely versatile material for paths, steps, and patio slabs. The process is described in some detail on pages 29-30 and 37-38, along with suggested proportions for appropriate cement, sand, and stone mixes.

One of the advantages of *in situ* concrete is its versatility – you can leave it as it is or top it with paving bricks, slabs, or tiles to create a more sophisticated finish.

Concrete can also be pigmented or screeded with pigmented mortar. Pigment powders are available in several colors, including red, green, and ocher. A simple way to apply it is to mix about 1 pound of the powder with about 2 pounds of cement (or a larger quantity in the same proportion) and sufficient water to make a paste. Trowel this over the surface and smooth it with a wooden float or steel plasterer's trowel. A little of the color will wash out with time, but a slightly mottled surface can be quite attractive.

Alternatively, you can color the concrete or the screed, but you will need large quantities of pigment to get any color intensity. If you do wish to color the concrete, you will need to add 10-30 pounds of pigment per cubic yard of concrete; if you color the mortar for the screed, add 16-50 pounds of pigment to each cubic yard of concrete, depending on the intensity of the color you are aiming for. Another rather simpler method is to sprinkle the dry pigment onto the wet screed or concrete and then work it in well with a plasterer's trowel. For this method you will need 1-2 cups (4-8 ounces) of powder per square yard.

If you prefer to leave the concrete its usual gray color, it can be artificially aged by brushing on a little yogurt to encourage moss and lichen to grow. Take care, though, as a mossy walkway is potentially dangerous, so only treat risers and areas of a patio which will not take heavy foot traffic.

Another interesting innovation is imprinted concrete, which creates the effect of cobblestones, fieldstone, or bricks. Special equipment is required to create the imprint, so it is generally best laid by contractors.

FORMWORK (SHUTTERING)

When casting concrete yourself, you will have to erect formwork for any structure which is to extend above ground. This applies to all staircases, but not necessarily to paths or slabs that are built with their upper surface at ground level.

Both the curved path and the steps featured here were built with shuttering. Ordinary softwood planks were used in the construction of the five 24-inch wide steps, while pliable hardboard (masonite) was used for the pathway.

The height of the risers and depth of the treads will depend on the slope of your garden. In this case they are 5 1/2 inches high and 14 inches deep. Refer to the instructions on page 40 and adapt the measurements to suit your requirements.

MATERIALS

The mix used for this step-by-step project is of medium strength, and suitable for paths, steps, and slabs that are exposed to weathering. The ratio used is 1:3:3 by weight, which means that each 100-pound bag of cement is combined with 300 pounds each of sand and 3/4-inch crushed stone. If a smaller 1/2-inch or 1/4-inch stone is used, the ratio should be altered to 1:3:2.

Instructions are included here for mixing by hand. If you are going to use a concrete mixer, follow the guidelines given on page 37.

1 Assemble a simple profile to establish how many steps will fit the slope of your garden (see page 40.) Decide more or less where you would like the steps to begin and end, and knock a peg into the ground at the top point and a longer post at the bottom.

2 Set a 2x4 at the base of the peg and mark the point where it meets the post positioned on the lower part of the slope. For accuracy, it is essential that the straightedge remain level, so use a spirit level to ensure you have the measurements right.

3 Measure the distance from the ground to the mark on the post, i.e. the total change in level. Then measure the distance between the post and the peg to establish the depth of the slope. Use these figures to decide how many steps to build.

4 Peg out the remaining corners of the stairway. The two new pegs should be 24 inches away from the peg and post already in the ground. Check that the outside corners are at 90°, using a steel measuring tape and the 3:4:5 method (see page 35).

5 Stake out all five steps, spacing them as required. The pegs are positioned at 15¼-inch intervals, and the steps themselves will be 14 inches deep and 5½ inches high. Use flour, chalk, or cement to mark the position of the treads on the ground.

6 Before excavating excess dirt, remove any turfs of grass which may be re-used somewhere else in the garden. It is not necessary to dig out all the soil. If you dig carefully, you can create a rough stairway which will be a good guide for the formwork.

7 The wood you use for the formwork must be straight, not bowed or warped, although it need not be new or clean. It is important to cut the upper edges neatly and absolutely straight as the concrete will be leveled off against the top edge of the wood.

8 The formwork must also conform to the dimensions of the treads and risers. Measure each piece and then nail all the pieces together, using a combination square for accuracy. If you cut the ends to form a point, it will be easier to knock them into the ground.

9 Position the formwork along the sides of the excavated staircase and knock it firmly into the ground with a club hammer. Ensure that the horizontal surfaces of the formwork remain level by checking them with a spirit level.

10 Since the formwork will be your guide for leveling the surface of the concrete, which will form the tread of the step, use a spirit level across the width of the steps to check that the sides are level with one another. Adjust if necessary.

11 It is also vital that the two pieces of formwork stand perfectly vertical. There should be a very slight slope from the back of each tread down to the front. Check all planes with a spirit level before you begin to mix the concrete.

12 Once the sides of the formwork are straight and secure, nail boards between them to contain the concrete which will form each of the risers. If there are any gaps at the sides, these will also have to be closed off with timber.

13 Now compact the sub-base of the steps with a punner or heavy post. If a layer of hardcore or crushed stone is to be included in the structure, it must be placed below the level of the formwork, or the loose material will be exposed once the formwork is removed.

14 Once all the formwork is in place you can mix the concrete. Choose a clean, dry, flat surface which will not result in moisture being absorbed from the mixture into the ground. Measure out the sand first and tip it out onto the mixing surface.

15 Now measure out the cement, using the same container to ensure that the proportions are correct. The ratio of cement: sand should be 1:3. Then mix the cement and sand with a spade or shovel until you achieve a consistent color.

16 Make a small crater in the center of the dry mixture and add water slowly. There is no need to measure the water, but it is important not to add too much or the concrete will be too liquid. Rather work gradually and add a little more once you have mixed it in.

17 Shovel the dry materials from the outside of the crater into the center. Take care that the water does not run out as you are mixing. Aim for a pliable mixture which is neither too watery nor too stiff. Add more water, a little at a time, if necessary.

18 Add the crushed stone to the mixture last. Measure it out in the container used for the cement and sand (see page 46 for proportions) then spread it evenly over the surface of the wet mixture. Continue to shovel until all materials are thoroughly combined.

19 Before you pour the concrete into the form, moisten the bare earth. This will prevent water from being absorbed from the concrete into the earth. Transport the wet concrete in a builder's wheelbarrow and then shovel it with a spade, filling each step.

20 Cut a straight length of 2x4, just long enough to cover the width or depth of each tread. Use it to compact the concrete with a chopping movement to get rid of any air bubbles, and then level it to the upper surface of the form, using a sawing motion.

21 Allow the concrete to set thoroughly for about 24 hours before removing the shuttering. First, carefully prise the planks away from the front of each riser, using a screwdriver. Then pull the two side sections out of the ground.

22 If you wish, lay pavers over the top of the treads. First position them loosely over the concrete to see how they fit, and then mix mortar in a cement: sand ratio of 1:5. Lay them as described on page 39, using a trowel to fill the joints with mortar.

23 Once the steps are complete, you can lay the path. You will need pegs and string or a builder's line to mark out its position. Use additional pegs where it curves, and measure the width at various points to ensure that the edges are parallel to each other.

24 Use flour or chalk to make more distinct lines on the grass, then carefully remove the turfs between them. Excavate the pathway to a depth of 4-6 inches to accommodate a 2-inch layer of gravel or crushed stone (hardcore) and 2-4 inches of concrete.

25 Compact the ground well with a punner or heavy pole and then pour in the hardcore. Distribute it evenly with a spade or rake, then compact it well. This will form the sub-base for the path, so it is vital that it is stable and there are no air-pockets.

26 Cut hardboard or any other suitable flexible material to the depth of the concrete, and nail to pegs to form shuttering. You can re-use the upright sections of the step formwork if you wish. Position the formwork and hammer it in place.

27 Make sure that the tops of both sides of the shuttering are on an even plane, allowing for a very slight drainage slope across the path. A gradient of 1:40 is ample in this context. Do not forget to use a spirit level to check the alignment.

28 Instead of mixing the concrete on a flat surface and then transporting it to the site, you could mix it in a builder's wheelbarrow for convenience. Follow steps 14-18, adding a little more water if you find that the mixture is too dry.

29 Spray the compacted hardcore base lightly with water before you tip the contents of the wheelbarrow between the shuttering. Shovel it evenly, so that it completely fills the formwork next to the bottom step. Mix another batch and repeat.

30 Use a 2x4 to compact and level the concrete. As you chop into it, water will rise to the surface. When the concrete has set, remove the formwork. Keep the concrete moist for several days to allow it to cure, hosing it every few days if necessary.

Whenever a patio and path are built at different levels, you will need to link them with steps. If you have used brick paving as the surface material, it usually looks best if you build the steps from the same brick.

Three steps, built into the slope, link this path and patio. Each step is built on a concrete foundation, while the paving is laid on compacted sand. On some sites, it may be necessary to excavate and lay hardcore or gravel to stabilize the sub-base.

For continuity, the risers of the steps are built in stretcher bond and the paving in the equivalent running bond. The paving is laid at a slight gradient (a run-off of 1:40 or 1:50 is recommended) to allow rainwater to drain away.

MATERIALS

A combination of ordinary facebricks and clay pavers has been used for this garden layout. Since they were obtained from the same supplier, they match in both color and texture.

The paving for both the path and the patio is laid on plastic sheeting. This is an optional step, but it stops vegetation from growing up through the paving, although it does not prevent seeds from sowing themselves between the bricks. There is also a school of thought which strongly opposes the use of plastic under flexible paving (where the bricks are jointed with sand) on the grounds that it prevents water from draining away and may cause moisture movement.

1 Start by establishing where the top and bottom step should be built. Measure both the horizontal and vertical lengths and make a simple profile (see page 40). Then cut away the general shape of the number of steps required from the soil.

2 Each tread is about 14 inches deep and 40 inches wide. Mix concrete in the required ratio (see page 30) and lay a 2-inch concrete foundation, a little larger than the first tread. When it has set, lay one course of the thinner paving bricks on mortar.

3 Mix another batch of concrete and fill in behind the first tread up to the level of the first step. This will form the foundation for the second step. Use a plank to compact the concrete, expel all air bubbles, and level the surface, then allow it to set thoroughly.

4 Each 7/8-inch inch high riser is built up with two facebrick courses and a single course of pavers, which also forms the surface of the tread. Use a corner block and builder's line to keep each course straight and lay the bricks using stretcher bond.

5 The top of the third step should be level with the surface of the patio. Build a one-brick wall and lay a single row of pavers on top as a header course. Fill the gap behind the step with concrete, level the concrete, and leave it to set.

6 Peg out the area to be paved, then remove all vegetation, and level the site, using the top step as a guide. You may need to excavate to allow for a 1-2 inch bed of sand. If the soil is unstable, you will need to allow for a sub-base of hardcore as well.

7 If necessary, spread hardcore and compact it well. Ensure that the surface slopes slightly away from the building (see page 36.) If you are using plastic sheeting under the paving, lay it now, overlapping the edges by 8 inches. Secure with bricks.

8 Lay two adjacent sides of the edging, setting the paving bricks in a bed of mortar. Use a spirit level to check that they are level and a steel builder's square to ensure that all corners are at right-angles. A line will help to keep the edging straight.

9 You will need to bed the paving bricks on fairly coarse, clean building sand which is free from stones and vegetable matter. Spread it over the plastic so that it is more-or-less level with the mortar that holds the edging in place.

10 Use a straight-edged length of timber to smooth and level the sand. If the patio is large, you will not be able to smooth out the entire area at once. Work in manageable sections and use a spirit level regularly to check the gradient.

11 Start laying the pavers, working systematically from the edging to the other side. Decide which paving pattern to use and then push each paving brick firmly into the sand. Make sure they are level, and use a rubber mallet to tap down any that protrude.

12 Now you can excavate the path. First mark the line it will follow with pegs and string, ensuring that the sides run parallel to each other. The steps are 40 inches wide, so a good width for the path is 36 inches. Loose-lay a few bricks to check the width.

13 Level and compact the area then lay plastic sheeting down. Lay the edgings on mortar first, making sure they are the same distance apart along their whole length – in this case about 18 inches, to accommodate four bricks laid side-by-side.

14 Fill in between the edgings with about 1 inch of sand as before and use a straightedge to flatten and smooth it. Then lay bricks in running bond. When all the bricks are in place, trim the plastic with a sharp utility knife and remove the scrap pieces.

15 Lastly, brush fine sand into the joints. Alternatively, brush in a 1:6 cement:sand mix instead, spray the surface lightly with water, and make sure that all traces of mortar are removed (see page 53 for how to remove hardened mortar if it dries).

This patio is built alongside a house, and raised above ground level, incorporating a low retaining wall along the front and a short flight of brick steps leading to the front door. Although the construction of the retaining wall and basic patio structure is not shown in the step-by-step photographs, the entire area was filled with several cubic feet of hardcore consisting of broken bricks, stones, and gravel. This was well compacted before the paving was laid. If the garden is level, preparation will be the same as for the patio illustrated on pages 50 and 51. If a retaining wall is to be built, use "brickforce" (a wire reinforcing mesh sold in rolls) on every third or fourth course, and make sure that there is adequate sub-surface drainage (see pages 35-36.) If the wall is any higher than 48 inches, consult an architect or engineer for specifications.

It is essential that the surface of any patio built adjacent to a house be located at least 6 inches below the underside of the interior floor slab, floorboards, or the top of the plastic damp-proof membrane (if there is one.) The steps, which lead to the house, are built up from a flat surface, so a single slab is thrown and the steps

are built on top of this. The gap behind each riser wall is filled with hardcore.

Since in this case the patio was bounded on three sides by existing walls, no edging was necessary. However, it was essential to insert a drainage pipe in the wall to cope with excess rainwater. If your patio is freestanding, you will need to lay an edging of some sort (for instance bricks set in mortar, as illustrated on page 51), and the drainage outlet will not be necessary.

1 If the patio is to be built above the level of the ground, build retaining walls and fill the area with hardcore and gravel. Use a punner or ramming tool to compact the entire surface, or use a compacting machine to speed up the operation.

MATERIALS

The steps are built with facebricks and matching pavers laid in a stack bond, although to save costs, ordinary stock bricks may be used on the inside of the steps where they will not be visible (see pages 28-29 for quantifying bricks and pavers.) The same paving bricks, laid in a neat basketweave pattern, are used to pave the surface of the patio. Coarse building sand is used to bed the bricks, and a fine sand to joint them.

2 The sub-base must be level before you can pave over it. Aim for a gentle gradient of about 1:40 to allow water to run off the finished surface. Use a spirit level to check the slope at several points along the width and length of the patio.

3 Peg out an area about 60 x 48 inches for the foundation slab of the steps and excavate to a depth of 2 inches. Mix concrete and lay it as described on pages 37-38. When it has set, mark out the steps with chalk, checking that the corners are at 90°.

4 Lay a stepped one-brick wall on one side, using facebricks for the outside skin and plaster bricks for the inside. Lay the first course on mortar, pressing the bricks down firmly. Spread more mortar on top, make a furrow with a trowel, then lay the next course.

5 Mark the position of the top tread, and then lay a half-brick wall, in stretcher bond, along the full width of the step. Scrape off excess mortar as you work. You do not need to use facebricks for the first four courses as they will not show.

6 Repeat the process, building three half-brick walls to form the risers. String a line along the front of each one as you work; this will help you to ensure that the brickwork is straight. Use a spirit level regularly to make sure that each wall is level.

7 Although the top course or two of each wall should be built with facebricks (the number of courses depending on the height of the riser), any bricks can be used for the lower courses. Complete these walls and both side walls and allow the mortar to set.

8 Fill the spaces behind the risers with broken bricks, crushed stone, gravel, and dirt. Compact this hardcore well, making sure that there are no air-pockets. Water lightly before topping with a thin layer of weak mortar, mixed in a 1:6 cement:sand ratio.

9 Mix a new batch of mortar in a 1:4 cement: sand ratio and lay paving bricks on the wet mortar already on the tread. Butter one end of each paver as you work, and use a trowel to fill any gaps which may be left. Scrape off the excess mortar.

10 Before the mortar dries, sprinkle dry building sand over the treads and use a sponge to wipe the cement off the surface. Mortar will stain, and if dry it can only be removed with spirits of salts (hydrochloric acid) or a weak solution of muriatic acid.

11 You can now pave the patio. Spread a 1-2-inch bed of sand over the entire area. Flatten and level it with a straightedge (see page 51), or make a punner from a block of wood and a batten, and tamp the sand down firmly to compact it.

12 Decide on a pattern before you start laying the pavers. Begin at a wall (or edging) and lay the bricks very slightly apart. Tap them firmly into place with a rubber mallet and check regularly with a spirit level that you are sloping the surface correctly.

13 It is essential to lay a drainage pipe to prevent rainwater from collecting on the surface. Knock a hole in the retaining wall and insert a length of 4-inch PVC pipe right through it. Use a little mortar to secure it and to patch the hole.

14 When all the paving bricks are in place, spread fine sand over the entire surface and sweep it into the joints. Hose the surface down lightly and then repeat, to make sure that there are no gaps. If the sand settles over time, add more later on.

PLAN 1   **TIMBER TREADS**

A very simple cast concrete stairway is transformed by affixing lumber at the front of the treads and pushing round river stones into wet mortar at the back of the treads and on the risers. The steps are constructed using forms, as shown on pages 46-49, but the use of hollow retaining blocks simplifies construction and helps to stabilize the embankment before the concrete is placed. If you are building on a steeper or longer slope, you will need to extend the stairway. Here, the path slopes gradually from the top of the fifth tread, and materials specified will enable you to lay five steps and 80 inches of pathway.

MATERIALS
15 x 17 x 13½ x 9 inch
  hollow retaining blocks
737 pounds cement (about
  682 pounds for concrete
  and 55 pounds for mortar)
2970 pounds or
40 cu inches sand
2750 pounds or 38 cu.
inches stone
12 x 60 x 8 x 2 inch
  hardwood planks
72 x ³⁄₈ x 3 inch coach
  screws
river stones
scrap lumber and nails
  for formwork

1 Measure and peg out a line 60 inches wide across the base of the slope where the bottom step is to be.
2 Excavate five rough steps in the embankment, ensuring that the upper surface extends backward about 16 inches to accommodate the tread, and that the steps are each about 6 inches high.
3 Compact and level the soil for the bottom step. Position three blocks across the width of the excavated tread with the 17-inch rounded section in front.
4 Compact and level the soil and position the blocks for the rest of the steps, then compact and level the path area.
5 Erect a 8-inch deep formwork to contain the concrete for the stairway, and a 2-inch deep one for the path.
6 Drill six holes in each piece of lumber and screw in the coach screws so that at least 1 inch of the head and shaft protrudes.
7 Mix concrete in a cement: sand: stone ratio of 1:4:4 and place it along the path. Then cast the concrete for the stairs, starting from the top step and placing it around and in the hollows of the concrete blocks.
8 Before the concrete sets, position planks along the path and at the front of the treads, pushing the coach screws firmly into the concrete. Leave overnight.

9 Mix mortar in a 1:4 cement:sand ratio and fill in the gap between the timber and the riser of each step. Then spread mortar to cover the surface of each riser. Press river stones into the wet mortar.
10 Allow to set thoroughly before removing the formwork.

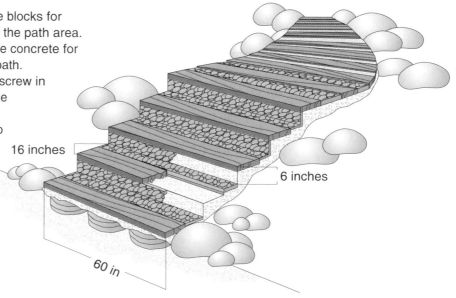

16 inches

6 inches

60 in

Expansive brick steps invite one to walk at a leisurely pace from one level to another in the garden. Two 60 x 32 inch planters at the top of the steps, one on either side, are rendered and painted to add contrast and interest to the structure, and also incorporate light fittings. These planters, like the steps themselves, are topped with flat-faced bricks, although pavers could be used instead. The materials specified are sufficient for six steps, rising up a 18 foot 4 inch wide slope, but if you wish, the stairway could be extended at either end if the site is suitable.

MATERIALS	Planters
Steps	790 bricks
519 bricks	880 pounds cement (about
462 pounds cement (154	308 pounds for the
pounds for foundations)	foundations)
1430 pounds or	286 pounds lime
20 cu. inches sand	3575 pounds sand
154 pounds lime	1232 pounds stone
792 pounds stone	2 x weatherproof light
880 pounds fill, soil, or sand	fittings with conduit
	(optional).

1 Measure out and peg a sloping area about 18 foot 4 inches wide and 88 inches long from top to bottom.
2 At the lowest point, excavate an 18 foot 4 inch x 16 inch trench to a depth of about 2 inches.
3 Dig away the bank immediately behind the trench to form a rough step. Then fill the trench with concrete mixed in a 1:4:4 cement:sand:stone ratio and allow to set.
4 Lay a row of bricks 2 inches in from the front of the foundation slab to form a stretcher course.
5 Fill in behind the bricks with soil or sand, leaving space for a 1-inch layer of concrete, measuring 14 inches from front to back, on top. Compact the soil before laying the concrete

to form a foundation for the front of the second tread.
6 When the concrete has set, lay bricks to form the tread as illustrated.
7 Build a two-course wall in stretcher bond to form the next riser so that the top of the first course of bricks is at the same height as the top of the first tread.
8 Repeat steps 3, 5, 6, and 7.
9 Build the third step the same way. Then build the next two steps 120 inches wide, centering them on the lower steps.
10 Dig away the slope on either side of the two 120-inch wide steps and excavate an area of about 56 x 36 inches to a depth of 2 inches below the top of the third step.
11 Erect formwork to prevent the bank from collapsing.
12 Place a few bricks in the center of the planter to create drainage holes. Then mix concrete in a cement: sand: stone ratio of 1:4:4 and spread evenly over the entire area to a depth of 2 inches.
13 Allow the concrete to set overnight, but remove the bricks before it hardens too much.
14 To construct the planters, build up one-brick walls five courses high to form rectangular "boxes."
15 Leave a gap in the front of the outer course to accommodate the light fitting, if required. Get an electrician to complete or check the installation before doing any further work.
16 Now build the riser of the top step as for the previous steps.
17 Render the exposed, outer surface of the planters using a 2:1:8 cement: lime: sand mix.
18 When the mortar has set, lay bricks around the top of the planters and along the top tread.
19 Fill the base of both planters with broken bricks and stones, then fill with dirt and plant.

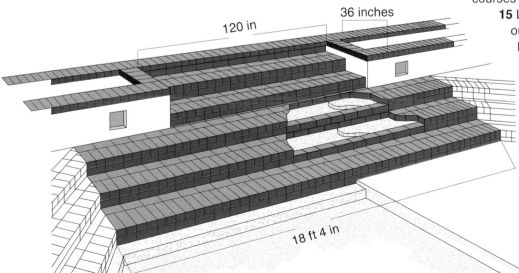

36 inches
120 in
18 ft 4 in

This lovely, random stepping-stone path, leading to beautifully overgrown brick steps, beckons one to explore more of the garden. Created with ordinary precast concrete slabs, the path is well planted with ground cover which softens the effect and give it life and color. The path widens as it nears a brick patio (not included in this plan.) Materials specify sufficient bricks, cement, sand and aggregate for the steps, the retaining wall on both sides of the steps, and an additional 80 inches of wall along the front. You will also be able to build a pathway which is about 140 inches long and covers a total of 240 sq. inches. The design can easily be enlarged so the stepping-stones create an informal patio.

MATERIALS
Steps
144 bricks
132 pounds cement
550 pounds sand
40 pounds lime
220 pounds stone

Walls
288 bricks
495 pounds cement

77 pounds lime
1958 pounds sand
hardcore for drainage

Walkway
1782 pounds crushed stone
  or hardcore (optional)
890 pounds sand
33 x 16³/₄ x 16 inch round
  slabs

1 Mark out and excavate the steps, roughly cutting out the general shape required (see pages 46-49.)
2 Lay a concrete foundation, 56 inches x 9¹/₂ inches in area and 2 inches deep, for the bottom step. (A 1:4:4 mix will use 55 pounds of the cement.) Leave to set.

3 Lay the first course of bricks, with a stretcher course in front and header course behind.
4 Then lay the second course with the header course in front and stretcher course behind.
5 Fill in behind the first tread with concrete to create a second 56 x 9¹/₂ inch foundation, 2 inches deep and level with the top of the first tread. Allow to set.
6 Build up all four treads in the same way. Allow the mortar to set thoroughly.
7 Dig away the soil along the sides of the steps. If necessary, erect formwork to prevent the soil from collapsing.
8 Dig foundation trenches 10 inches wide and 4 inches deep. Mix concrete in a 1:4:4 mix using 330 pounds of the cement specified, and fill the trenches. Allow to set.
9 Lay a one-brick wall in stretcher bond along the sides of the steps and extend the walls, if necessary, along the front.
10 Once the mortar has set, fill behind the wall with hardcore to aid drainage.
11 Level the area where the pathway is to be laid and compact the earth well.
12 Spread a 4-inch layer of hardcore and compact it again.
13 Cover the hardcore with a 1-2 inch layer of sand.
14 Lay the slabs, ensuring that they are flat and level.
15 Fill the gaps between them with good quality soil and plant with a suitable ground cover.

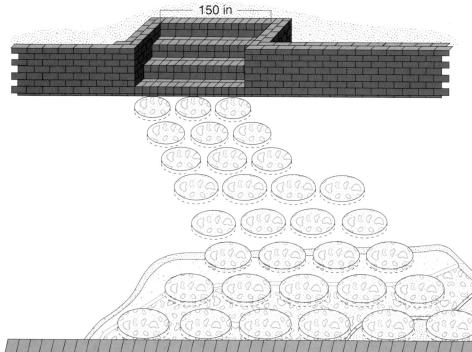

150 in

These charming rustic steps are set at the base of a grassy bank and link a stone patio/walkway with a slightly raised garden. Made from wooden ties and split poles which have been sunk well into the ground, they are built along the same lines as the adjacent split-pole retaining wall and rustic planters. Materials specified will enable you to build four steps set into a similar slope, and a simulated stone slab patio or walkway of 40 sq. feet. If you cannot find poles that are long enough to span the treads, simply abut two shorter ones to fit, and adjust any of the dimensions to suit your site.

MATERIALS
Steps
4 x 40 x 8 x 6 inch timber or precast railroad ties

1 x 108-inch split pole, 3½ inches in diameter

1 x 83-inch split pole, 3½ inches diameter

2 x 72-inch split poles, 3½ inches diameter, for the sides

1 x 1.44 m split pole, 3½ inches in diameter

1 x 36-inch split pole, 3½ inches in diameter

36 x 16-inch split poles, 3½ inches in diameter

78 x 12-inch split poles, 3½ inches in diameter

78 x 3-inch anodized nails

Patio/walkway
24 cu. inches sand

23 x 20 x 20-inch reconstituted stone slabs

23 x 20 x 20-inch reconstituted stone slabs

23 x 10 x 10-inch reconstituted stone slabs.

1 Excavate the area of the steps, cutting away roughly to the shape required.

2 Dig an 8-inch deep trench along the front and set thirty 12-inch long split poles in place. Nail the 108-inch long pole (or two 54-inch poles) to the back of these, so that the upper surface of all the lumber is straight and level. Fill in the excavated soil in front of the step and compact it well.

3 Dig an 8-inch deep trench on either side of the steps, following the slope of the ground. Position the first six or seven 16-inch long poles on either side.

4 Dig another trench at the back of the first tread (which should measure 19½ inches from front to back), then set the next row of poles in place to form a second riser. Nail the 83-inch long pole behind this row as before, fill the trench, and compact the fill.

5 Continue, systematically building each tread, making sure the risers are level and well secured from behind. When all the side poles are in place, secure these in the same way. Fill in the treads with soil, leaving 7 inches for the railroad ties and a bed of sand, and compact them.

6 Spread a 1-inch layer of sand on top of the soil before positioning the ties.

7 Top up the area around and between the ties with good quality soil before planting.

8 When the steps are complete, level the ground where the patio or walkway is to be sited , and compact it well.

9 Spread 1-2 inches sand over the surface and water it lightly with a hose to aid compaction.

10 Lay the slabs in a random fashion, ensuring that they are level.

11 Fill the gaps with good soil before planting.

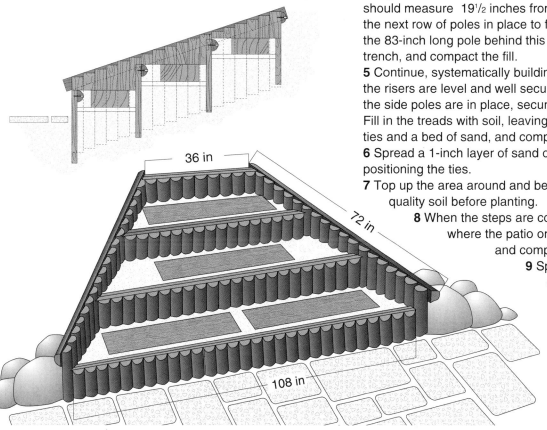

36 in

72 in

108 in

Railroad ties and bricks are cleverly combined to create a slightly winding, gradually stepped path leading to an informal garden. These materials are laid on a concrete slab which is stepped up the slope. Materials listed will enable you to construct a walkway about 16 feet 8 inches long; the number of steps you decide to build will depend largely on the gradient of your site. If wooden ties are not available, hardwood planks or precast concrete imitation ties could be used instead. Although most of the ties will stay in place without bolts or screws, it is a good idea to secure those on the treads firmly in the concrete with coach screws.

MATERIALS
230 bricks
495 pounds cement (297 pounds for foundation)
2596 pounds sand (594 pounds for bedding bricks)
1177 pounds stone
11 x 92 x 8 x 6 inches railroad ties
33 x 4-inch coach screws (optional)
scrap lumber for formwork

1 Mark the line of the walkway and excavate an area 2-4 inches wider than the path on either side and 8 inches deep. Use formwork where the foundation is stepped and overlap the levels of concrete by at least 2 inches.

2 Mix the concrete (materials listed are for a 1:4:4 ratio of cement, sand, and stone) and place it over the entire excavated area to a thickness of about 2 inches.
3 If you wish, insert about three coach screws partway into the underside of each tie, ensuring that the head and at least half of the screw protrudes from the lumber.
4 Before the concrete sets, position the ties about 1½ inches part along the path and at the front of each tread and push each one down firmly to level it.
5 Once the concrete has set thoroughly, lay the bricks between the ties in the pattern illustrated. Bed each section of paving on enough sand for the bricks to lie flush with the sleepers – about 1¾ inches. Lay the bricks side by side as shown, cutting to fit the curves of the path where necessary.
6 Sprinkle a very weak, crumbly mixture of cement and sand (mixed in a 1:6 ratio with a little water) over the surface to fill in any gaps.
7 Spray the walkway lightly with water before this mortar dries.

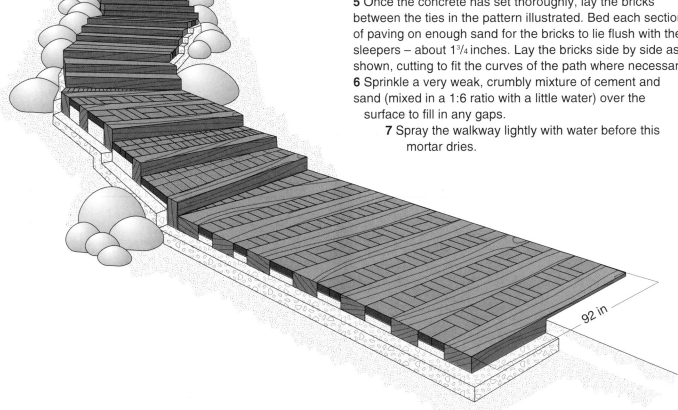

92 in

This small, simple, and very practical patio area alongside a boundary wall is linked to the house by a small, gradual flight of steps. Similar to the steps and patio featured on pages 52-53, the project requires only basic skills. Although facebricks and pavers are specified throughout, ordinary stock bricks could be used where brickwork is not visible, just as they are in the step-by-step project. If you need to build more than three steps, or if you want a patio bigger than 48 sq. inches, you need to adjust the quantities.

MATERIALS
Steps
123 facebricks
198 paving bricks
308 pounds cement (123
  pounds for concrete and
  176 pounds for mortar)
1232 pounds sand

528 pounds stone
88 pounds lime (optional)

Patio
540 paving bricks
1782 pounds bedding sand
fine sand for jointing

1 Peg out an area of 100 x 60 inches for the steps.
2 Excavate to a depth of 2 inches and compact the soil to create a firm sub-base.
3 Mix concrete in a cement: sand: stone ratio of 1:4:4 and throw the foundation slab. Compact, level, and leave it to set.
4 Chalk out the area of each step before laying stepped side walls. Build up two courses for the first two steps and five for the top, using a 2:1:8 cement: lime: sand mix for the mortar.
5 Now build the back and front risers by laying two walls between the side walls, five and two courses high respectively.
6 Allow the mortar to set, then fill the two cavities with broken bricks,

stones and soil or sand. Compact so that the material is about 10 mm below the top of the bricks.
7 Top the fill with about 10 mm concrete.
8 Lay pavers over the lower surface.
9 Lay a stretcher course of bricks on the paving to form the middle riser. Fill in with bricks and a 10 mm layer of concrete, then top with pavers as before.
10 Finally lay pavers to cover the top tread.
11 When the steps are complete, level the ground in front of the steps and compact it well.
12 Spread a 25-50 mm layer of sand over the compacted area, then compact and level it.
13 Lay pavers in a running-bond pattern, working away from the wall.
14 Set edgings in mortar.
15 Spread fine sand over the surface and sweep it in to fill all gaps between the bricks.

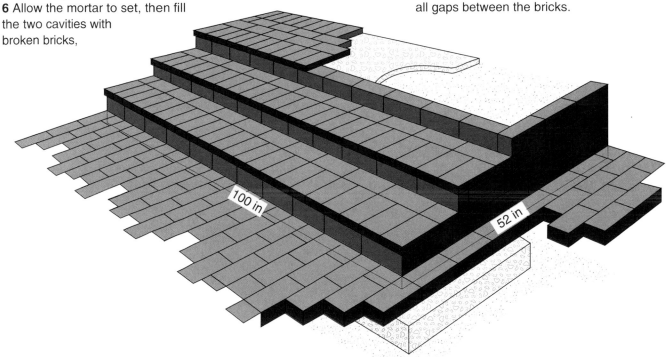

100 in

52 in

Well-coordinated brickwork is the key to this attractive entrance area which features low walls, a paved walkway, a planter, and two flights of steps, one of brick, and the other cast concrete with a tile finish. The site slopes slightly, and the elements can easily be adapted to many sites. Although this is a relatively complicated project, it does not require any special building skills. The secret is to tackle it systematically. Each element should be marked out before construction begins, and brickwork should be completed before the surfaces are paved and tiled. The materials listed will enable you to build the planter, both sets of steps, a 32 x 88-inch landing at the top of the steps and a 12-inch long pathway. Bricks for the patio are laid in the same way as the path. Quantities specified will cover about 80 sq. inches.

MATERIALS

Foundations
495 pounds cement
2266 pounds sand
2266 pounds stone

Tiled steps
539 pounds cement
2178 pounds sand
2178 pounds stone
187 x 8 x 8 inch ceramic
  floor tiles
33 pounds cement-based
  tile adhesive
4 kg grout

Brick steps
384 facebricks
130 kg cement
115 pounds sand
115 pounds stone

Planter
720 facebricks
396 pounds cement
198 pounds lime
1595 pounds sand

Walls
260 facebricks
198 pounds cement
99 pounds lime
803 pounds sand

Path & patio
1,125 paving bricks
2376 pounds bedding sand
33 pounds cement
132 pounds sand for edging
fine sand for jointing

1 Peg out the entire area marking steps, planter, and walls as shown on the illustration.
2 Excavate foundation trenches, allowing for slabs of at least 4 inches under the steps and planter, and 6 inches for walls.
3 Mix cement, sand, and stone in a ratio of 1:4:4 and place concrete in all the trenches. Put a few bricks in the base of the planter to create drainage holes. Allow concrete to set, but remove bricks before it firms thoroughly.
4 Build tiled steps first. Dig away a rough stairway and set formwork in place.
5 Mix concrete and place in the formwork, then allow it to set.
6 Mix mortar in a 2:1:8 ratio and build up the planter in stretcher bond.

7 Now build the brick steps. Start in front, ensuring that the back row of bricks lines up with the planter and proposed position of the front wall. Lay all on edge as illustrated, starting with a stretcher course in front.
8 Lay a second course over the first, this time starting with a header course; the two courses will form the first tread.
9 Lay the second and third steps in the same way.
10 Build one-brick side walls for the path in stretcher bond. Finish the tops with a header course of bricks laid on edge.
11 Clear the area to be paved and compact the ground.
12 Spread a 1/4-1/2 inch layer of sand over the entire area; compact and level it.
13 Lay edgings against steps and walls. If the patio does not abut a wall, lay an edging in mortar along one side.
14 Lay bricks in a herringbone pattern, cutting them last.
15 Lay the rest of the edgings in mortar.
16 Spread fine sand over the surface. Brush into the joints.
17 Finally, spread tile adhesive over the concrete steps, lay the tiles, and grout them.

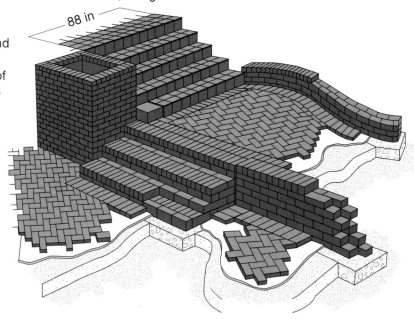

This well-proportioned stairway steps up gradually at right angles. Bricks are laid on edge in a basketweave pattern and the steps are held in place by a header course of bricks placed on edge at the front of each tread. Risers are constructed by building up two stretcher courses in the usual way. The amount of paving laid at the top of the steps may vary between sites. The quantities given here will allow you to pave about 320 sq. inches. An attractive 80 x 48 inch planter edges one side of the stairway, and matches an existing 52-inch high facebrick wall. If you wish to build a wall as well as the steps and planter, you will need extra bricks, cement, and sand, and stone for the foundations.

MATERIALS

Steps
900 paving bricks
1000 pounds cement (340 pounds for foundations)
4044 pounds sand
1375 pounds stone

Planter
670 facebricks
550 pounds cement (55 pounds for foundations)
253 pounds lime
2222 pounds sand
440 pounds stone

1 Peg out the edges of the area where you plan to build the steps. Then measure and mark an area of approximately 72 x 28 inches where the lowest step will be built.
2 Excavate about 2 inches from the bottom step, then fill with concrete mixed in a cement: sand: stone ratio of 1:4:4. Level and compact it and allow to set.
3 Lay a header course of bricks 2 inches from the front of the slab, and a stretcher course along the right-hand side.
4 Now dig away the bank immediately behind this first tread, at the back and on one side, roughly forming the second tread. Excavate to the height of the header course.
5 Mix more concrete and place behind the header course and in the excavated section to create a foundation for the second step.

6 When the concrete has set, lay two header courses along the front of the second step to form the required right angle. Lay two stretcher courses on the right-hand side.
7 Lay the paving over the first tread, setting bricks on edge to form a basketweave pattern. End with a brick-on-edge header course at the front.
8 Repeat steps 4 through 7.
9 Repeat these steps a second time, but this time throwing a concrete slab for the upper section of paving rather than another tread. Pave the upper area using the same pattern.
10 Dig away the slope to the right of the steps, excavating a foundation trench for the planter about 2 inches below the bottom step.
11 If the earth is soft, erect formwork to prevent the bank from collapsing.
12 Place a few bricks on end in the center of the planter to create drainage holes. Then mix the concrete in a 1:4:4 ratio and place to form a foundation slab.
13 Allow the concrete to set overnight, but remove the bricks before it hardens too much.
14 Construct the planter by building up one-brick walls to form a rectangular box 11 courses high.
15 Lay a header course of bricks on edge around the top of the planter.
16 Place broken bricks and stones in the base of the planter, then fill with soil and plant.

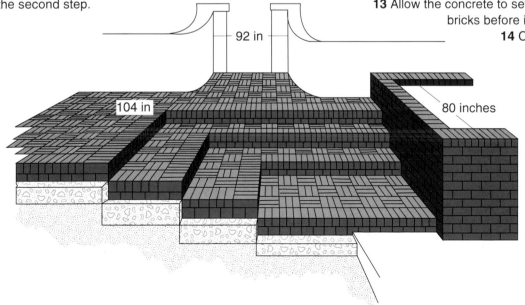

92 in

104 in

80 inches

An attractive flight of steps built from dressed stone slabs allows a gradual descent from one level of the garden to another. The lower section of the steps spreads out from a central landing topped with fieldstone. A water feature (not included in the project) adds charm and character. You could continue the stairs across the full width of the area, or you could construct a stepped planter in place of the water feature. A precast pond could also be positioned in between the two lower flights. The stone you use to build the steps will depend on what is available in your area.

MATERIALS

94 slabs of cut stone, average size 12 x 8 x 4 inches, or stone slabs to cover 320 sq. inches

fieldstone to cover about 80 sq. inches

90 bricks

572 pounds cement

(385 pounds for concrete and 66 pounds for brickwork)

2310 pounds sand

1540 pounds crushed stone

plywood and scrap wood for formwork

2 x precast concrete lamps (optional)

1 Use a profile to establish where the steps will be located. Peg out the area.

2 Roughly excavate the stairway.

3 Construct the formwork in three sections, with treads about 8 inches deep and risers about 4 inches high. Use plywood wherever curves are required. Hammer into place,

leaving the central landing untouched.

4 Compact the earth within the formwork. Mix concrete in a ratio of 1:4:4 (cement: sand: stone) and place it to form the foundation slabs for the steps. Level and compact the concrete and allow it to set thoroughly.

5 Excavate the earth between the two bottom flights of steps, using formwork to prevent the bank from collapsing.

6 Dig a trench between the two bottom stairways, 12 inches wide and 4 inches deep, for the foundation of the front wall of the landing.

7 Mix concrete in a 1:4:4 ratio using about 22 pounds cement. Place in the trench and allow to set.

8 Build a one-brick wall six courses high in stretcher bond at the front of the landing, leaving drainage holes at the base. Allow the mortar to set thoroughly, then render the front of the brickwork. If you are building a water feature, construction may also take place at this stage.

9 Remove the formwork and backfill the gap behind the wall with crushed stone and soil.

10 Excavate and flatten the earth on the landing. The surface should be level with the base of the concrete which forms the bottom step of the top flight, and the top of the concrete which forms the top step of each lower flight.

11 Mix another batch of concrete and place on the landing. Level it, compact it, and leave to set.

12 Lay the stone slabs to form the steps, working from the bottom step. If they do not fit exactly, fill in the gaps with mortar or smaller pieces of stone.

13 Lay the fieldstone in mortar on the landing.

14 If you are installing lamps, have an electrician do the wiring, then concrete them in place at the top of the steps.

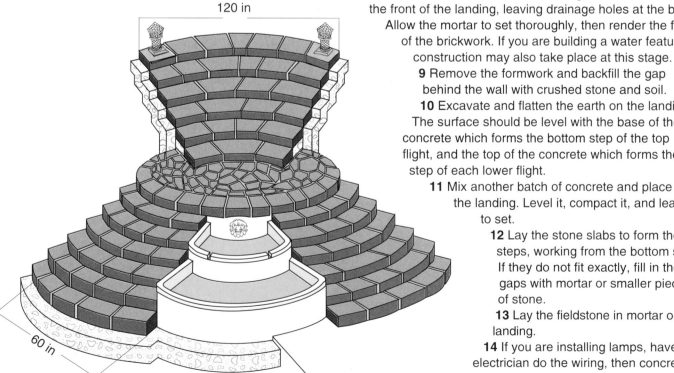

120 in

60 in

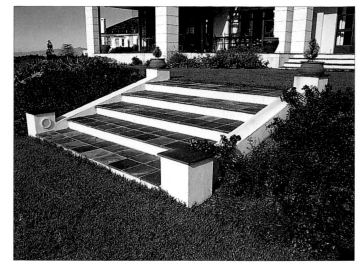

A formal garden staircase, which is a feature in itself, has been rendered and painted and the treads topped with attractive slate tiles to blend with the architecture of a large house. Relatively deep 24-inch treads combine with minimal risers up the slight slope. Although the project specifies $11\frac{1}{2}$ x $3\frac{3}{4}$ x $3\frac{3}{4}$ inch concrete blocks, the steps may be built with bricks or blocks of a different size. If you need to adapt the materials, some of the other materials and the proportions may vary. You may also prefer to tile the treads with ceramic, terracotta, or quarry tiles. All are suitable provided they have a matte, non-slip finish. If lighting is to be incorporated, you will need to employ the services of a professional electrician.

MATERIALS

190 x $11\frac{1}{2}$ x $3\frac{3}{4}$ x $3\frac{3}{4}$ inch blocks (some broken)
385 pounds cement (about 165 pounds for foundations and 154 pounds for rendering)
110 pounds lime
1540 pounds sand

660 pounds stone
100 x 12 x 12 inch slate tiles
4 x 20 x 20 inch slate tiles
44 pounds cement-based tile adhesive
2 x sealed light fittings with conduit (optional)

1 Peg out the 160-inch-wide staircase, marking the position of the two front pillars.
2 Dig two $19\frac{1}{2}$ x $19\frac{1}{2}$ inch foundation trenches, 2 inches deep, for the pillars, and a 120 x $7\frac{1}{2}$ inch trench of the same depth for the wall which will form the first riser.
3 Mix concrete using a cement: sand: stone ratio of 1:4:4 and place in the holes. Allow to set. If lighting is to be installed, set conduiting in place before placing the concrete.
4 Build the two lower pillars five courses high and lay the two courses of the bottom step in stretcher bond, about 2 inches in from the edge of the concrete.
5 When the mortar has set, cut away the earth behind to form a rough second step.
6 Dig a second foundation trench for the next riser wall and fill it with concrete.
7 Once the concrete has set, fill the gap between this and the front wall and compact the fill so that the surface is about 1 inch below the top of the front bricks. Top with concrete.
8 Repeat this procedure for each riser, building up the side walls at

the same time.
9 Build two more pillars at the top of the steps.
10 Use broken blocks to fill in the slope of the walls between the top and bottom pillars. Allow the mortar to set.
11 If light fittings are required, install them or have them fitted now.
12 Render the side walls and risers with a 2:1:8 mixture of cement, lime and sand.
13 When the rendering has set, tile the treads and the top of the pillars. Grout the tiles with a little mortar.

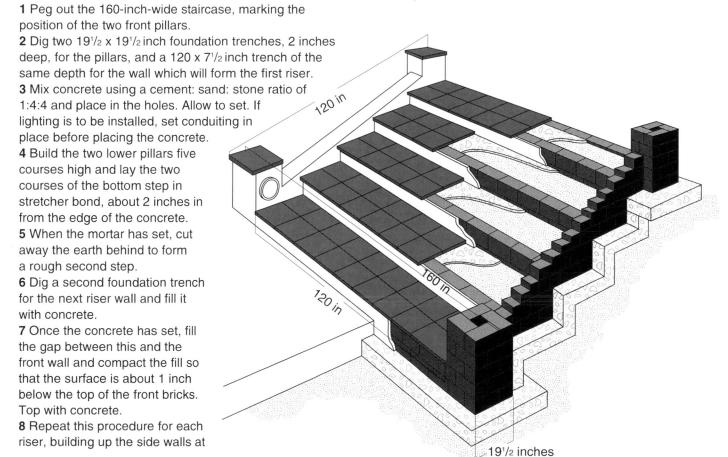

120 in

120 in

160 in

120 in

$19\frac{1}{2}$ inches

U.S. CUSTOMARY/METRIC CONVERSION TABLE

To convert the measurements given in this book to metric measurements, simply divide the figure given in the text by the relevant number shown in the table alongside. Bear in mind that conversions will not necessarily work out exactly, and you will need to round the figure up or down slightly. (Do not use a combination of metric and U.S. customary measurements – for accuracy, stick to one or the other system.)

TO CONVERT	DIVIDE BY
inches to millimeters	0.0394
feet to meters	3.28
yards to meters	1.093
sq inches to sq millimeters	0.00155
sq feet to sq meters to	10.76
sq yards to sq meters	1.195
cu feet to cu meters	35.31
cu yards to cu meters	1.308
pounds to grams	0.0022
pounds to kilograms	2.2046
gallons to liters	3.785